Teacher Strikes and the Courts

Teacher Strikes and the Courts

David L. Colton
Edith E. Graber
Washington University, Saint Louis

LexingtonBooks
D.C. Heath and Company
Lexington, Massachusetts
Toronto

The original data reported in this book were collected in conjunction with a grant from the National Institute of Education to the Center for the Study of Law in Education at Washington University, Saint Louis. However, nothing herein necessarily reflects the views or policy of the sponsoring agency, and no endorsement should be inferred.

Library of Congress Cataloging in Publication Data

Colton, David L.
  Teacher strikes and the courts.

  Bibliography: p.
  Includes index.
  1. Strikes and lockouts—Teachers—United
States. I. Graber, Edith E. II. Title.
KF3450.T43C64   344.73′0189283711   81–47887
ISBN 0–669–05121–7   347.304189283711   AACR2

Published simultaneously in Canada

Printed in the United States of America

International Standard Book Number: 0–669–05121–7

Library of Congress Catalog Card Number: 81–47887

Contents

Preface and Acknowledgments

The courts are among the least understood of all our public institutions. Charged with the task of resolving disputes both mundane and momentous, the courts are veiled by elaborate procedure, specialized language, and behind-the-scenes consultations and maneuvers. Seeking understanding, we ponder the appellate courts' published opinions, trying to fathom their roots and their implications. Biographies probe the minds and lives of the attorneys and judges who manage the litigation process. Movies, television, and the press provide glimpses of the real or imagined world of law firms, jury rooms, courtrooms, and cases. Dawnings of awareness and comprehension develop, but then some social crisis or issue erupts, and the principal actors are faced with the task of deciding whether to take the matter to court. It is then that the limited scope of our understanding becomes manifest. Enough is known to anticipate some of the consequences of litigation. Not enough is known to predict with confidence the likelihood of these consequences, their costs and benefits, or their significance for the issue at hand. Yet decisions must be made.

School boards must make decisions when teachers strike, as they have been doing with increasing frequency in recent years. Should the teachers be taken to court? Why or why not? If so, when? How will the other side respond? What will the court do?

In this book, we describe how school boards decide whether to go to court, how teacher associations defend themselves in court, and what judges do. The book is based on data collected in the context of legal proceedings accompanying teacher strikes in the late 1970s. Through interviews with dozens of the key actors in these dramas, our case studies of court proceedings, and a survey of school districts experiencing teacher strikes during 1978–1979 we obtained a wealth of descriptive information. *Teacher Strikes and the Courts* is in significant measure a report, in their own words, by the key actors involved in strike-related litigation. This book serves to remove mystery, to enlighten, and to provide a basis for informed action. School-board members and teacher-organization leaders should find this book informative and useful.

Although bounded by the data on which we relied, the book suggests a broad view of the role of the courts in resolving social disputes. The disputes that the courts address do not originate in court; they originate in society. The courts do not seek out issues; parties must bring issues to court. But the courts will not accept social disputes in their raw form. The legal issues embedded in a social dispute must be abstracted from it; only then can they be presented to a court. Thus, although intimately connected, the dispute in court and the dispute in society are not the same. Their differentiation and their simultaneous existence are significant. The evolution of each dispute affects the other. Judges know this; attorneys know, too. In this book we show how this knowledge affects the process of dispute resolution. Students of the legal process, and of the relationships between law and society, should find this book instructive.

Acknowledgments

The individuals who made the most important contributions to this book must remain anonymous. They are the dozens of school-board attorneys, teacher attorneys, school-board officials, teacher-organization officials, and judges who took time from their busy schedules to talk with us, to complete our questionnaires, and to direct us to further sources of information. In this book, we honor those people by relying extensively on their own words. As we learned from our sources, so, we hope, will our readers. If this book teaches, it is because we were taught by the many who cooperated with our study.

Our investigation of teacher strikes and court proceedings was made possible by a grant from the National Institute of Education and by the hospitable environment provided by Washington University. Our project officers in Washington, D.C., and our colleagues at Washington University provided encouragement and fostered our efforts. The following individuals read drafts of the manuscript and offered helpful advice: Susan Appleton and Merton Bernstein of the Washington University School of Law and Kenneth Dolbeare of the University of Massachusetts at Amherst. Of course these organizations and individuals are absolved of all responsibility for what we report here.

A large number of Washington University students assisted us in gathering data. Here we can do no more than list them by name and express our thanks, along with the hope that some useful learning may have come from the experience. Thank you, Mary Ann Campbell, Martha Clevenger, Jo Ann Donovan, Alan Frelich, Bruce Goldstein, Pat Greenfield, Denise Hartsough, Ilene Lanier, Randal Lemke, Bonnie Reid, Alan Tomkins, and Dan Willett.

Bobbe Winters managed the logistics and aggravations of manuscript preparation with skill and grace.

The work reported here is the product of a genuine collaboration between the authors. We share the responsibility for what follows.

1 Introduction

In the 1950s teacher strikes were mere curiosities, occurring so infrequently that most policymakers rightly dismissed them as accidents or aberrations unworthy of close analysis. However, in the 1960s the incidence and impact of teacher strikes increased sharply. Whereas the number of teacher strikes averaged only three per year in the 1950s, by the first half of the 1970s they were occurring at a rate of more than 130 per year. In 1979–1980 there were 242 teacher strikes—an all-time high.[1] Few communities have been immune. Strikes have disrupted schools in lush suburbs near Chicago, quiet Yankee towns, old central cities of the Northeast, dynamic new cities in the South and West, and rural communities across the land. Many strikes have lasted for weeks.

A teacher strike requires some sort of response from local school officials. Often the response is to take the matter to court. The transfer is accomplished by petitioning for an injunction ordering teachers to refrain from striking. However, boards frequently find that the remedies issued by the courts are ineffective, that they involve unsought judicial intervention in the dispute that initially triggered the strike, or that they aggravate rather than alleviate the board's problem.

This book explores what happens when teacher strikes are transferred to court, why they are met with varied and unexpected judicial responses, and why all the parties—school boards as petitioners, teachers as respondents, and judges as decision makers—often voice dissatisfaction with the injunctive process and its outcomes. Our central thesis is that the parties present judges with fundamentally incompatible conceptions of the nature of the teacher–board dispute. School-board attorneys contend that the problem before the court is an illegal strike. The task of the court, therefore, is clear and straightforward: to ascertain whether a strike exists or is imminent, to find that it is illegal, and then to issue an injunction. But teacher attorneys contend that the significant problem is the labor–management dispute that triggered the strike in the first place. An injunction would not address this underlying problem and could even exacerbate it. What is needed, teacher attorneys suggest, is negotiations, not injunctions.

The court thus is presented with two problems. One is a strike; the other is a labor–management dispute. To accept the board's position is to address the strike issue but to ignore the underlying dispute. To accept the teachers' viewpoint is to condone illegal action. Neither option is wholly satisfactory. Faced with this dilemma, judges react in diverse and unpredictable ways. Some focus on the strike, acting on injunction requests on legal grounds alone. Some delay the injunctive process, hoping that the underlying dispute somehow will be resolved. Others actively intercede, seeking to mediate or otherwise expedite settlement of the underlying dispute. Occasionally a court dismisses the entire matter, leaving the board and the teachers to resolve their problems elsewhere.

Such actions raise broad questions about the role of courts and the rule of law. Should a court deal solely with the narrow legal question immediately before it, or should it attempt to address the underlying social dispute? Should a court intercede on behalf of settlement efforts? Should it do so even over the objections of petitioners? Should a court issue injunctive relief if it is likely that teachers will not comply with the order of the court? Should a labor–management dispute be before the court at all? Although this book does not provide definitive answers to such problems, it does explore the nature of the issues upon which the formulation of public policy and practice can be based.

The Dispute at the Bargaining Table

Most contemporary teacher strikes are associated with collective-bargaining disputes. Collective bargaining is a relatively recent development in public education. In the 1960s, unhappy about their own unmet needs and inspired by unionized blue-collar workers' gains in wages and working conditions, teachers began a campaign to introduce collective bargaining to the field of public education. Initially most boards of education resisted teachers' demands for bargaining. School boards viewed collective bargaining as a threat to established patterns of accommodation with teachers. The traditional pattern was predicated on the assumption—embodied in law—that school boards are responsible for determining teachers' wages and working conditions. It also was built on a norm—embraced by the ideology and the professional associations of most educators—that school boards dealt with teachers individually, not collectively. Disputes over wages and working conditions ultimately were resolved unilaterally rather than bilaterally, by declaration rather than by negotiation.

Despite board reservations, bargaining and bargaining-like practices have become widespread in public education. Beginning with Wisconsin in 1959, one state after another adopted statutes permitting or requiring the practice. By 1980 a majority of state legislatures had authorized some form of teacher–board bargaining[2] (see appendix). In many other states teacher–board bargaining is widespread even in the absence of specific legislative authorization.

One feature of private-sector collective bargaining—the right to strike—has not been widely accepted in the schools. In private employment the right to strike is thought to be an essential concomitant of bargaining. Bargaining presumes the existence of equivalent power on both sides of the table. When negotiation fails to produce a settlement, employees have a choice to make. They can continue to work under whatever terms are offered by management. Or they can strike, hoping that the pressures brought by a work stoppage will break the impasse. Management in turn can acquiesce to worker demands or can resist the strike by withholding wages and by continuing operations. Labor legislation adopted in the 1930s and 1940s legitimated the right to strike.

Whatever its merits in the private sector, the right-to-strike principle has rarely been extended to teachers. Despite widespread acceptance of teacher–board bargaining, only seven states had adopted right-to-strike laws by 1980. In each of these states the right applied only under carefully circumscribed conditions that, if not met, rendered a teacher strike illegal. Twenty-three states had statutes prohibiting teacher strikes. In states without legislation the courts, when asked, have almost always ruled that teacher strikes are illegal in the absence of legislative authorization.

The fact that most strikes are prohibited virtually invites legal remedies. A board can take the matter to court, requesting an injunction ordering the teachers to refrain from illegal activity. In some states such requests are mandatory. However, in most states boards must decide whether to seek such relief. Some boards simply accede to teacher demands in the face of a strike. Other boards countenance strikes in hopes that a settlement can be achieved without court action. Usually, however, neither concession nor delay constitutes an adequate response to the several pressures that boards face. To yield to the teachers is to jeopardize the budget and to cede the control that most board members feel they are legally and morally obliged to exercise. Delay angers the parents and students who are most immediately affected by a strike. Consequently, the court option is an attractive one.

But going to court puts the focus on only one aspect of the dispute. If judicial relief is sought, the strike no longer is simply an extension and escalation of the labor–management dispute heretofore handled at the bargaining table. Rather, the strike is made the basis for a legal dispute.

The Dispute in Court

Until the 1930s labor injunctions were widely used as tools for fighting strikes in the private sector.[3] Management attorneys found that they could easily obtain injunctive relief, often without the other side's having an opportunity to be heard in court. On the strength of management claims that a strike would irreparably harm a legally protected interest such as commerce or property, a court would issue an order temporarily banning initiation or continuation of a strike. Failure to abide by such orders subjected violators to contempt-of-court proceedings and possible fines or jail sentences. Thus union leaders and workers who had engaged in preparation for a strike suddenly found they were confronting not only their employers but the majesty and power of the courts as well.

Union leaders launched a campaign designed to secure legislation that would prevent "government by injunction." Eventually the campaign brought victory. The Norris-LaGuardia Anti-Injunction Act of 1932 and similar legislation in many states curtailed the courts' capacity to issue injunctive relief in labor–management disputes. Unable to rely on the assistance of the courts, corporate managers learned to bargain more successfully and to cope with strikes when bargaining led to impasse.

But the anti-injunction statutes did not apply to public-sector strikes. In the 1920s and 1930s, the idea of public-employee strikes was simply not tolerated. Calvin Coolidge had won the presidency largely on the basis of his widely publicized actions and words against the Boston police strike. "There is," Coolidge told Samuel Gompers, "no right to strike against the public safety by anybody, anywhere, any time." Even as stalwart a labor supporter as Franklin Roosevelt proclaimed that public employees must not strike.

Strikes occurred anyway. A flurry of work stoppages by teachers and other public employees immediately after World War II prompted several state legislatures to adopt statutes providing stiff penalties for public employees who engaged in strikes. In other states judges adopted positions similar to those of the legislatures. A leading case arose in Norwalk, Connecticut. In a declaratory-judgment action, the state's supreme court asserted that government is "run by and for all the people, not for the benefit of any person or group," that public-employee strikes were incompatible with this principle of government, and that case law "uniformly upheld" the right of a government to injunctive relief from employee strikes.[4]

In the 1950s, when most public employees were distinctly nonmilitant, there were few occasions to invoke antistrike statutes or labor injunctions against public employees. Among teachers there were only twenty-six strikes from 1950 to 1959.[5] They were isolated incidents, not harbingers of things to come.

In 1962 a strike by New York City teachers ushered in a new era of public-employee militancy in education and other sectors of public employment. The strike eventuated in a handsome settlement for teachers. Significantly, however, the strike was terminated on the afternoon of its first day when strike leaders complied with an injunction.[6] Thus there were two lessons. One was that militance paid off. The other was that strikes could be ended by injunction. In the 1960s, bellweather strikes in New Jersey, Kentucky, Indiana, California, Michigan, and elsewhere were met by school-board requests for injunctive relief.[7]

After 1965, as teacher strikes became more commonplace, so did school-board efforts to utilize injunctive relief. Thus teacher strikes constituted not only an emerging social phenomenon but also a new category of legal phenomena. Published accounts of strikes invariably indicated that injunctions were a regular part of board strategy.[8] "Strike-management manuals," which circulated among school managers, indicated that resort to the courts was an option available to boards. In the 1970s injunctive relief was sought in about 40 percent of all teacher strikes.[9] The proportion is higher if one-day strikes and those in states with limited right-to-strike laws are excluded.

When school boards resort to injunctive relief, striking teachers face a special set of problems. An injunction threatens to shift the focus of attention from the bargaining table to the courtroom, from issues of wages and working conditions to issues of legality. To return to work in the face of an injunction is, in effect, to abandon the purpose of the strike, for an employer has no particular incentive to yield on disputed issues if the work of the organization is being carried out. Yet to defy an injunction is to risk substantial sanctions not merely with respect to public opinion but also with respect to such tangible legal matters as fines and even jail sentences.

To avoid these problems, teachers, through their attorneys, utilize whatever legal tactics they can muster in order to delay or deflect injunctions and, where possible, to turn the injunctive process to their own advantage. These courtroom goals are not ends themselves; rather, they are means toward the larger end of achieving satisfactory settlements at the bargaining table. The task, in different terms, is to blunt the injunctive process to the extent necessary for teacher negotiators to achieve a settlement.

The task of teachers' attorneys is not an easy one. As Bohannan has observed, the courts are designed to "(1) disengage the difficulties from the institutions of origin which they now threaten, (2) handle the difficulty within the framework of the legal institution, and (3) set the new solutions back within the processes of the nonlegal institutions from which they emerged."[10] When the board initiates an injunction proceeding, it is attempting to accomplish the sort of disengagement cited by Bohannan. If the teachers seek to block disengagement of the strike from the bargaining dispute, they must do so within the substantive and procedural requirements of law. They must find ways to introduce law and evidence that will persuade a judge that the issue is broader than that of ascertaining whether a strike is legal.

In this book we will be particularly concerned with the nuances and consequences of the fact that parties in injunction proceedings present courts with a legal dispute—the strike—that is inextricably embedded in a larger labor–management dispute. Judicial management of the relationship between the disputes raises fundamental questions about judicial efficacy and equity. These questions have implications that go beyond the immediate issues.

Teacher strikes constitute not only an emerging social phenomenon but also a new focus for social research. This book draws on the authors' recent study of the injunctive process in teacher strikes.[11] We conducted field studies of teacher strikes in California, Illinois, Louisiana, Michigan, Missouri, New York, Pennsylvania, Vermont, and Washington. There we spoke with petitioners, respondents, and their legal counsel. We studied trial-court records and appellate cases. We interviewed officials representing teacher associations, school-board associations, and state labor-relation and education agencies. We analyzed court rulings and statutory law pertaining to injunctive relief from teacher strikes. In addition, we conducted a survey of all 158 districts experiencing teacher strikes in 1978–1979.[12] We also consulted the few available studies of legal proceedings accompanying teacher strikes.

Chapter 2 examines the nature and origins of the disputes that develop between school boards and teachers. Chapter 3 reviews the nature of the injunctive process. It also provides a case account of an injunction hearing, illustrating the processing of a teacher strike in the courtroom. In the three following chapters, we examine the actions of the parties involved in the injunctive process: boards as petitioners, teachers as respondents, and judges as decision makers. Chapter 4 looks at the options school boards weigh in determining their response to the strike and at the legal processes and strategies that boards employ in the courtroom. Chapter 5 notes the techniques that teachers as respondents use to delay, evade, or capitalize on injunction proceedings. Chapter 6 describes the pressures that may induce judges to employ restraint, delay, and mediation as they attempt to deal with the strike, the underlying dispute, or both. The last chapter presents a critique of public policies that rely on courts as forums for ending teacher strikes.

Notes

1. *Government Employee Relations Report* (Washington, D.C.: Bureau of National Affairs, July, 21 1980)871:18.
2. *Cuebook II: State Education Collective Bargaining Laws* Report No. F80-5 (Denver: Education Commission of the States, 1980).
3. Arthur A. Sloane and Fred Witney, *Labor Relations,* 3rd ed. (Englewood Cliffs, N.J.: Prentice-Hall, 1977), ch. 3.
4. *Norwalk Teachers' Association v. Board of Education,* 83 A.2d. 482, Sup. Ct. of Errors of Ct. (1951).
5. Robert J. Thornton and Andrew Weintraub, "Public Employee Bargaining Laws and the Propensity to Strike: The Case of Public School Teachers," *Journal of Collective Negotiations in the Public Sector* 3 (Winter 1974):34.
6. *The New York Times,* April 12, 1967, p. 1.
7. Martha Clevenger, "Teacher Strikes: 1960–1968," mimeographed (Saint Louis: Center for the Study of Law in Education, Washington University, 1980).
8. For examples, see David L. Colton, "The Influence of an Anti-Strike Injunction," *Educational Administration Quarterly* 13 (Winter 1977):47–70; Donald J. Noone, *Teachers v. School Board* (New Brunswick, N.J.: Institute of Management and Labor Relations, Rutgers University, 1970); Robert G. Stabile, *Anatomy of Two Teacher Strikes* (Cleveland: EduPress Publishing, 1974); and Christopher R. Vagts and Robert B. Stone, *Anatomy of a Teacher Strike* (West Nyack, N.Y.: Parker, 1969).
9. A national survey of strikes at the beginning of the 1975–1976 school year showed that 43 percent of the districts sought injunctive relief. See David L. Colton, "Why, When and How School Boards Use Injunctions to Stifle Teacher Strikes," *American School Board Journal* 164 (March 1977):32–35. A national survey of 1978–1979 strikes showed that 40 percent of the districts sought court relief. See Edith E. Graber, "Survey of 1978–1979 Teacher Strikes," mimeographed (Saint Louis: Center for the Study of Law in Education, Washington University, 1980).
10. Paul Bohannan, "Law and Legal Institutions," *International Encyclopedia of the Social Sciences* 9 (1968):73–78.
11. The research was supported by the National Institute of Education, through grant no. NIE-G-78-0149. Findings are reported in David

L. Colton and Edith E. Graber, "Enjoining Teacher Strikes: The Irreparable Harm Standard," mimeographed (Saint Louis: Center for the Study of Law in Education, Washington University, 1980).

12. Strike sites were identified from information provided by the Bureau of National Affairs, the Bureau of Labor Statistics, and selected state departments of education. For a full report of the survey, see Graber, "Survey of 1978–1979 Teacher Strikes."

2 The Underlying Dispute

Legal disputes do not begin in court. They begin in society. Yet the social origins of legal disputes may not be apparent in court. School-board petitions seeking injunctive relief detach the legal issues from the underlying social dispute by focusing solely on the teachers' strike. The unresolved teacher–board dispute that triggered the strike is ignored. Subsequent chapters will show how injunction proceedings sooner or later reestablish connections between the legal dispute and the underlying dispute. This chapter focuses only on the latter. The first portion of the chapter traces the development of teacher strikes and teacher militance in the United States. Attention then is given to the social forces that foster adversarial relationships between boards and teachers, to the channeling of those forces by the organizations to which teachers and school boards belong, and to the collective-bargaining process. The final section of the chapter characterizes the teacher strikes that occurred in 1978–1979; these strikes form one of the principal sources of data on which this book relies.

The Incidence of Teacher Strikes

The common school movement that began in the middle of the nineteenth century was institutionalized in ways that precluded militant conflict between teachers and school boards. The prototypical school district employed only one teacher. As recently as 1940 the average school district employed only nine teachers—far too few to create conditions conducive to collective conflict.[1] Conflicts were resolved within a bureaucratic pattern of control in which power resided at the top of the hierarchy. School boards and teachers were arrayed in a superior–subordinate relationship, and the superiors determined the outcome of conflicts. Buttressing the organizational structure was an ideology widely shared by teachers, administrators, board members, and the public: The schools were essential adjuncts of a democratic society, elected officials were responsible for managing school affairs, and teachers were professionals engaged to perform a public service.

The structure and the ideology of the common schools were reflected in the principal associations to which educators belonged. The dominant organization was the National Education Association (NEA). A confederation of state associations, it was all-inclusive, embracing classroom teachers, superintendents, curriculum specialists, and principals. Superintendents dominated the organization. The NEA strategy for improving public education stressed self-help, partly achieved through prestigious nonpartisan commissions that influenced the direction of public-school policy, and partly through pressure brought to bear on state legislatures.[2] State legislatures were viewed as the main source of the funds and the laws needed to improve the conditions of schooling and teaching. Rather than opposing each other in the state capitols, teachers and administrators collaborated to exert "professional" influence on legislators. The emphasis was on the provision of information. Educators pled the interests of children and carefully avoided the appearance of being an "interest group" such as a union or business association.[3] The American Federation of Teachers (AFT), with its roots in the national labor movement, urged a more militant approach to issues touching on teacher–board relationships, but few teachers subscribed to the AFT view. Neither the NEA nor the AFT endorsed the idea of teacher strikes.[4]

Thus it is hardly surprising that teacher strikes were rare and unlikely events. The few that occurred reflected unique circumstances rather than underlying militance. For example, a flurry of teacher strikes in the 1930s was prompted by missed paydays. A brief surge of strike activity in 1946–1948 stemmed from a combination of wartime demands and severe inflation.[5] The more typical pattern was apparent in the 1950–1965 period, when the number of teacher strikes averaged less than three per year.

In the 1960s the established pattern of teacher–board accommodation changed dramatically. In more and more communities teacher–board confrontations occurred. Strikes were called with increasing frequency. During the 1970s the nation experienced more than one-hundred teacher strikes annually.[6]

The Roots of Teacher Strikes

The increasing frequency of teacher strikes has prompted much inquiry and speculation. Most early investigations were issue oriented. These studies sought "explanations" for strikes in the immediate issues that triggered them: salaries, class size, evaluation procedures, and the like.[7] The Bureau of Labor Statistics (BLS) still reports data in terms of immediate issues.[8] But issue-oriented studies lack depth; they identify precipitating factors, not causes.

In recent years a substantial body of literature has developed, giving attention to more fundamental causes of teacher strikes.[9] This literature highlights three types of explanatory phenomena. The first explores the manner in which the social context of teaching, both outside and inside the schools, breeds militance. A second model stresses the process of interest mobilization whereby the disparate agendas of teachers and school boards are crystallized and then embedded in an organizational process that brings disputes into focus. The third looks to the dispute-resolution process—usually some form of collective bargaining—and to failures in that process. Each approach reveals dimensions of complexity not often evident in school-board petitions seeking injunctive relief from a teacher strike.

The Social Roots of Militance

Since midcentury several social forces have coalesced to heighten teacher and school-board militance. For teachers the principal concerns have been economic status and working conditions. School boards have tended to focus on problems of control, competence, and finance.

Teacher Concerns. Educators have long contended that teaching is an underpaid occupation not only in view of the imputed social significance of schooling but also in view of the incomes of comparably trained workers. In the 1950s and 1960s professional dissatisfaction with teacher wages was reinforced by developments outside the schools. The postwar baby boom, coupled with social demands for more years of schooling, created a serious shortage of teachers. In 1955 the prestigious Fund for the Advancement of Education reported that it would not be possible to attract and retain sufficient numbers of teachers unless there were dramatic changes in teacher-compensation patterns.[10] Concurrent with concern about the quantity of teachers, there was growing anxiety about the quality of teaching. Critics and reformers, bolstered by Russian successes in space and by the activist stance of the Kennedy and Johnson administrations, helped establish a climate conducive to sharp boosts in local, state, and federal spending for education.

By 1971–1972 teacher salaries, which had lagged behind those of the average worker until midcentury, were 20 percent higher than average worker salaries.[11] It is not clear whether the improvement is attributable to the increasing militance of teachers during the period or whether it was simply a by-product of school-district competition for scarce teachers. What is clear is that in the 1960s teachers became accustomed to gradual but steady improvement of their economic status in both absolute and relative terms.

In the 1970s teacher expectations for continued improvement were abruptly shattered. Enrollments stopped growing. Suddenly there was an oversupply of teachers. Chronic inflation eroded the purchasing power of teachers and other salaried employees whose contracts did not include automatic cost-of-living adjustments. There was public disillusionment with the efficacy of schooling and other forms of government enterprise. With the disaffection came a taxpayer revolt symbolized by California's Proposition 13. It struck directly at the property tax—historically the principal source of school-district revenues and hence of teacher salaries. By the late 1970s teachers were beginning to lose the salary gains that had been achieved in previous years. Between 1972 and 1979 the purchasing power of teachers' annual average salaries dropped nearly 9 percent.[12] Dissatisfaction grew apace.

Working conditions provide another source of teacher dissatisfaction. Early in this century a movement, which Callahan calls the "cult of efficiency," infused the thinking of school leaders and policymakers.[13] Inspired by then-current precepts about "scientific management," the movement stimulated school-district consolidations, which eliminated more than 80 percent of the nation's school districts. Today nearly two-thirds of the nation's teachers work in the 2,000 districts enrolling more than 5,000 students each.[14] A 5,000-student district employs upward of 200 teachers—too many to permit face-to-face contacts in which employers and employees can manage their disputes informally. Concurrent reforms designed to systematize school management produced quantification and depersonalization; decisions affecting teachers came to be based on staffing ratios, salary schedules, bulk purchasing, cost accounting, and output measures such as "credit hours," drop-out rates, and test scores. Students of industrial relations have repeatedly contended that such depersonalization prompts worker disaffection, dissatisfaction, and militance.[15] Such phenomena have become widely apparent in the schools. In the late 1960s tracts by Holt, Kozol, Herndon, and others portrayed the schools as impersonal and uncaring bureaucracies.[16] Teachers who have written about their willingness to strike repeatedly recite these themes.

Studies of the teaching profession also focus on teacher dissatisfaction. Lortie's portrayal of the teacher of the 1960s outlines two main components of what he calls teachers' "anatomy of discontent."[17] First, too much of their time is diverted to nonteaching tasks—clerical duties, nonclassroom duties, and externally imposed interruptions originating with parents, administrators, or other teachers. Second, teachers complain about interpersonal relationships: disruptive students, critical parents, unsupportive principals, teacher colleagues who refuse to carry out their fair share of chores. Corwin, approaching the problem from a different perspective, reached much the same conclusion as Lortie.[18] Professionalization of teaching, he found, breeds militance. Teachers find their professional discretion in managing instructional programs hindered by organizational arrangements requiring standardization, specialization, and centralized authority systems. The more professionally oriented teachers, Corwin found, have higher rates of conflict with school managers.

If conditions in the workplace leave something to be desired, they still may be tolerable if the workers believe that they are performing useful and valued work. However, in the 1960s and 1970s criticism of the schools—long a familiar feature of the educational enterprise—took on a new dimension. The competence of teachers began to be openly questioned. Reformers talked of "teacher-proof" curricula and technology-based learning systems. The competency-testing movement seemed to indicate that students were not learning basic skills. Surrounded by external critics, harassed by well-meaning reformers whose efforts often seemed to teachers to be shallow and ineffective, and daily faced by disrespectful students, many teachers longed for some form of support. The setting was ripe for initiatives from organizations that promised to improve salaries and to restore "dignity" to teaching.

School-Board Concerns. Social forces also have promoted school-board militance. At midcentury the position of school boards in the scheme of educational governance, while by no means clear or settled, was at least comprehensible. There was a hierarchy of authority that ran from the state constitution to the state legislature to the state education agency to the local school board to its superintendent, and from there through middle managers to the teaching staff and on down to students. While each level had some discretion, it was to be exercised within parameters set by higher levels. However, starting in the 1950s new actors decisively entered the scene. The courts became increasingly active, not merely in the desegregation arena but also in supporting the exercise of rights demanded by teachers, students, and parents. Congress and the U.S. Office of Education in the 1960s assumed major significance in educational policymaking and financing. Particularly in large cities, where the community-control movement was focused, groups heretofore ostensibly represented by the established school boards demanded decision-making rights of their own. And teachers, using their newly militant language and techniques, demanded roles as equals rather than as subordinates in the establishment of wages and working conditions. Threatened with encroachment on all sides by groups insisting on influence but still bound by established custom and laws, boards became much more sensitive to issues of control.[19]

Incongruously, threats to board control were accompanied by simultaneous demands for the more vigorous exercise of control by school boards. Boards were charged with the task of implementing new policies in areas such as desegregation, special education, and career education. Popular demands for improved school performance became translated into expectations that school boards somehow take the steps necessary to ensure minimum competence among school children. Meanwhile off in the wings there were voices expressing doubts as to the capabilities of school boards, and the public schools themselves, to effectively address the problems.[20]

For a time, particularly in the 1960s, school boards were provided with substantial revenue increases to carry on the work of the schools. Local taxes, state aid, and federal financial assistance boosted educational spending at rates which exceeded rates of inflation and of enrollment growth. But then in the 1970s the upward trajectory of revenues leveled as federal deficits and local taxpayer resistance capped spending increases. Simultaneous enrollment declines had the effect of increasing units costs of schooling, as did efforts to improve schooling by reducing student-teacher classroom ratios. Energy costs skyrocketed, along with inflation-driven expenditures for supplies, capital equipment, and maintenance. Teachers' demands for improved salaries, fueled by the expectations based on salary gains in the 1960s, constituted one more demand on the school boards' increasingly limited financial resources. Hard decisions were required. In many cases they took the form of stronger resistance to teachers' salary increases and efforts to exercise more control over teachers' working conditions.

Interest Mobilization

Self-help is a familiar mode of response by individuals and groups seriously dissatisfied or frustrated. In the 1960s teachers dramatically strengthened their organizational capability to act collectively on behalf of their own agendas. School boards soon did likewise. Interest-mobilization activities became a second factor contributing to the increasing incidence of teacher strikes.

Militant Professionalism. Until the mid-1950s the idea that there might be a formalized adversarial or bargaining relationship between teachers and school boards or that teachers might act independently and militantly on their own behalf, was well outside the mainstream of popular and professional thinking. However, in the late 1950s Myron Lieberman and others engaged in a consciousness-raising venture that altered prevailing thought about the conditions of teacher employment. In the field of education, Lieberman said, analysis of collective action was dominated by clichés. He set about the task of demolishing them. He noted that doctors, the prototypical professionals, acted collectively through their national organization to control fees. Lawyers, through their professional association, specifically endorsed the idea of withdrawing from employment for "good cause." Teacher strikes would not necessarily be against children; they could be for children if teaching conditions were detrimental to learning. Moreover, teacher strikes could hardly be said to be threats to the public safety; strikes were symptoms of employee–employer problems rather than revolutionary threats to the regime. Thus, Lieberman concluded, the idea of teacher strikes should not be rejected on a priori grounds. The issue was a pragmatic one. And on pragmatic grounds, he suggested, it might be wise to give teachers the right to strike: "The added bargaining power gained by having the right to strike helps to prevent conditions of employment from deteriorating to the point where strikes are necessary."[21]

In other writings, Lieberman focused on the issue of bargaining. The NEA, he felt, was not prepared to advance the interests of teachers via bargaining relationships because the NEA was an administrator-dominated organization. And the AFT was not properly constituted to mobilize large numbers of teachers. What was needed was a revamping of teachers' national and state organizations so that they could act effectively on behalf of professionalism in the schools.[22]

This self-help ideology was compatible with other ideologies developing at the same time. One ironically arose within the ranks of school management, where reaction against the excesses of scientific management was giving rise to language and techniques stressing "human relations," "participative decision making" and "collegial relationships." Teachers, according to the new rhetoric, should be partners in the decision-making process.[23]

Outside the schools the civil-rights movement demonstrated that direct action was a useful tactic in the pursuit of social justice. For a time it was possible for teachers to imagine that militant action on their part also promoted social justice, particularly in the large urban school systems where concentrations of minority children presumably would be the beneficiaries of improvements in teachers' salaries and working conditions. Although the possibilities for an alliance of teacher militants and civil-rights militants were wrecked by the 1968–1969 confrontations between teachers and community-control advocates in New York City, the language and tactics of direct action nonetheless became part of the rhetoric and action of teacher groups.

Coincidental with changes in teacher ideology in the 1950s and 1960s there was a series of crucial organizational events in New York City. In 1959 the New York City local of the AFT launched a campaign to organize the city's teachers. The national office of the American Federation of Labor (AFL), then worried about lagging union membership in blue-collar occupations and interested in promoting white-collar unionism, provided financial support for the organizing effort. Late in 1960 the AFT local organized a one-day demonstration on behalf of improved teaching conditions, and to call attention to its demand for a representation election. The school board subsequently held a referendum asking teachers whether they favored collective bargaining. They did. In December 1961 a representation election resulted in an AFT victory over NEA locals, which only belatedly recognized what was happening. The following spring, bargaining over the first contract reached an impasse on the salary issue, and a strike by 21,000 teachers shut down the school system.[24] The strike promptly was enjoined, and teachers returned to work after one day. However, in the ensuing negotiations, substantial salary improvements were obtained by the teachers. Moreover, no penalties were assessed against the strikers, despite the ostensibly automatic sanctions provided in New York State's antistrike Condon-Wadlin Act.

The New York City events demonstrated that teachers could be organized on behalf of economic issues as well as professional ones. The representation election—a key aspect of collective bargaining—provided a powerful vehicle for organizing teachers. And bargaining itself appeared to produce handsome gains without apparent costs to the teachers involved. Unionism and collective bargaining suddenly came to be seen as viable mechanisms for giving voice to teacher dissatisfaction. Unionism offered more than just a vehicle for seeking improvements in teachers' economic and working conditions. Unionism provided moral support, an outlet for expressing dissatisfaction with school policies and school management, and a sense of efficacy and power to teachers frustrated by the apparent unconcern and unresponsiveness of the established structure.[25]

At first the giant National Education Association was slow to recognize or respond to the challenge of the AFT. The language of unionism, the practice of collective bargaining, and the prospect of strikes ran counter to the history, ideology, and internal control structure of the NEA. However, teacher dissatisfaction could be ignored only at the risk of losing present members and potential members to the AFT. For a brief period the NEA experimented with its own version of techniques for channeling teacher discontent and rallying teacher membership.[26] Before long the NEA recast its ideology, drove out the administrators who had dominated it, and reorganized itself so as to compete directly with the AFT on behalf of an organizational structure geared to collective bargaining.

Beginning in the 1960s and continuing on through the 1970s NEA–AFT rivalry for membership was acute, particularly in metropolitan areas where representation elections could result in membership gains or losses of hundreds or even thousands of teachers. To a large extent, recruitment campaigns have turned on the question of which organization seems best able to bargain effectively on behalf of teachers.[27] Thus in communities where membership is at stake, the position of teacher bargaining teams often is affected not merely by the bargaining issues themselves but also by the presence of a rival unit that may be quick to point out any weaknesses in the bargaining team's achievements. In Saint Louis, for example, representation elections in 1974, 1975, and 1978 resulted in narrow victories for the AFT unit; one election was decided by a single vote.[28] A long strike in 1979 was prompted in part by AFT leaders' goal of establishing their supremacy more solidly.

For a time teachers seemed invincible in their drive for collective bargaining. The practice of bargaining spread rapidly. Teachers won gains at the bargaining table. Strikes appeared to be both feasible and successful weapons in the push for improved wages and working conditions. However, in the mid-1970s the momentum slowed. Although a majority of states had adopted statutes authorizing teacher–board collective bargaining, nineteen states still had no teacher bargaining statutes in 1980 (see appendix). Moreover, problems were encountered in the courts. The Supreme Court's decision in *League of Cities* v. *Usery* scuttled hopes for national legislation fostering teacher–board bargaining.[29] In a Hortonville, Wisconsin, case the U.S. Supreme Court sustained a school district's procedure for dismissing striking teachers.[30] Virginia's supreme court outlawed teacher bargaining in that state,[31] and Missouri's top court declared that a contract signed under the duress of a strike was void.[32] Moreover, teacher organizers proved to be fallible, as several key strikes ended ignominiously with trivial gains.[33]

Militant Management. School managers gradually developed counterstrategies. Most school-board members are elected laypersons who serve without pay on a part-time basis. Heavily middle class in background and outlook, few board members are personally acquainted with the details of labor–management relations or the process of collective bargaining and contract administration. Neither, for that matter, are many top administrators. In the 1960s initial management responses to teacher militance were dominated by sentiments of disbelief and indignation. However, it gradually became apparent that the militance was not a passing phenomenon and that the pressure for bargaining demanded more pragmatic managerial responses.

There have been two main lines of resistance. The first has been to resist bargaining itself. Bargaining is widely viewed by board members as a threat to traditional management prerogatives and responsibilities in the areas of finance, instruction, and policy. So believing, school managers and their associations lobby against statutes permitting bargaining, and they resist local teacher demands to engage in bargaining. Several teacher strikes have resulted from teacher–board disputes about collective bargaining itself rather than from unresolved disputes over contractual terms.

The second line of resistance has been to develop more effective bargaining strategies. An increasing array of bargaining aids is available to school boards. "How-to-bargain" manuals and "strike-management" manuals now are abundant. Professional negotiators are available for hire. Assistance is available from state and national associations of school boards and administrators.[34]

By the late 1970s increasing numbers of school boards became resigned to bargaining; attention began to shift toward mastery of techniques for resisting teacher demands at the bargaining table and for making counterdemands. This new focus was fueled, in part, by the social forces noted previously—heightened financial pressures on school budgets and public demands for improved performance in the classroom. In addition, boards came to recognize that strikes were not unmitigated disasters to be avoided at any cost. Management literature began to suggest that some strikes could be averted if teachers knew that boards planned to resist them and that strikes could even be won through skillful strike-management strategies.

The Bargaining Process

Outwardly, the collective-bargaining process is quite straightforward. Representatives of employees and representatives of management present proposals concerning wages and working conditions, negotiate in good faith to resolve differences, and then incorporate the agreed-upon terms in a contract that is mutually binding.

The realities of bargaining are more subtle and complex. Negotiation, like diplomacy, is not for amateurs. The process demands a thorough understanding of the issues themselves, as well as their implications for other issues and for the effectiveness of the organization. Client groups must give their negotiating teams enough discretion to make deals at the bargaining table but not so much that agreements reached will be repudiated at the ratification stage. Personality characteristics and behavioral styles also profoundly affect the success of the bargaining process.

In view of the complexity and delicacy of bargaining relationships, given the fact that many school districts have little or no experience with bargaining, and further given the scarcity of skilled practitioners of the process, it is hardly surprising to find that studies and reports of bargaining in public education are filled with instances in which the process has gone awry. For example, Cresswell and Simpson cite one district in which a board member participating on the bargaining team delivered what subsequently was called "the dog-food speech"; he informed the teachers that their demands for a cost-of-living increase exceeded the increases being received by other working people in the community and that the teachers thus could do like others, that is, eat dog food. In the ensuring strike, "dignity" was reported by the strikers as their number 1 reason for staying out.[35] Bendiner, reporting on an early strike in Ecorse, Michigan, notes that the board, reacting strongly, initiated dismissal proceedings—but then found that the consequences of following through were too egregious to manage; in the settlement that emerged, the teachers made substantial gains.[36] Mitchell et al., following their direct observations of the bargaining process in several districts, found that bargaining teams frequently misperceived the goals and tactics of their counterparts on the other side of the table.[37]

Of course, it is not simply the procedural difficulties of bargaining that trigger strikes. There are substantive issues too. Inherent in the bargaining process is a dynamic that requires the negotiation and allocation of any available values. Virtually anything is subject to being placed on the bargaining table: personnel evaluation, time for parent conferences, participation in textbook-selection committees, teacher–pupil ratios, rules for determining credit for salary advancements. As the bargaining relationship matures, it appears that more and more issues are negotiated.[38] Klaus describes how the issues evolved in New York City. The first contract focused on salaries, relief from nonteaching chores, and grievance procedures. In the next round of negotiations teacher proposals dealt with priorities for using available board funds, the school calendar, the assignment of teachers to special classes and duties, class size, and policies for dealing with difficult schools. To the teachers these matters, and particularly the last, were "working conditions" and hence negotiable. Management saw the items as administrative and not to be infringed by a contract. Mediation was required to avert a strike. In their third contract the New York teachers' union won the right to unilaterally administer the welfare fund established by the board. But negotiations for a fourth contract reached an impasse over the teachers' demands for expansion of union-endorsed compensatory education

programs, procedures for handling disruptive students, and several welfare issues. A three-week strike ensued.[39]

Nonbargaining Strikes

The preceding analysis has implied that all teacher strikes originate in
the constellation of factors involving teacher dissatisfaction, unionization,
and bargaining processes. However, some strikes have other origins. For
example, the New York City strikes of 1968–1969 grew out of a confrontation between community-control advocates and teacher-organization concerns about job protection. The issue was whether teacher
employment conditions were to be determined by the central board of
education with whom the teachers negotiated or by newly established
community boards.[40] Some strikes are more clearly aimed at state legislatures than at local school boards. Occasionally there are wildcat strikes
called over some grievance at the local building level; the resolution of
these strikes tends to be contingent on the resolution of the grievance
rather than on redefinition of contractual terms. Some strikes are simply
designed to demonstrate teacher concerns about noncontract items such
as program reductions; often such strikes are scheduled for only one day.
Nonbargaining strikes such as these are not unusual, but they constitute
only a small portion of all teacher strikes.

The 1978–1979 Teacher Strikes

The teacher strikes that occurred in the 1978–1979 school year reflect
the complexity and variety of underlying teacher–board disputes. There
were 158 strikes—more than had occurred in 1977–1978 but fewer than
would occur in 1979–1980.[41] Twenty-three states and the nation's capital
were affected. Strikes occurred in Frost Belt cities such as Cleveland and
Bridgeport and in Sun Belt cities such as Tucson and New Orleans. Small
communities such as Lower Snoqualmie (Washington) and Cairo (Illinois)
were affected, along with medium-size cities such as Fresno (California)
and Rockford (Illinois). Outside the cities suburbs such as Levittown
(New York), Warren (Michigan), and Hazelwood (Missouri) experienced
school shutdowns resulting from teacher strikes. Most of the Southeast,
along with the Plains and Mountain states, escaped strikes. The Northeast,
Midwest, and Pacific states fared less well. The existence of bargaining
statutes did not seem to make much difference; among the four states
with the highest number of strikes, two (Pennsylvania and Michigan) had
bargaining statutes whereas the other two (Ohio and Illinois) did not.

Collectively the 1978–1979 teacher strikes reflect the causes discussed in preceding sections of this chapter: developments within the larger society, the interest-mobilization process among teachers and school boards, failures in the bargaining process, and nonbargaining incidents.

Economic causes were particularly significant. Teachers had become increasingly frustrated by several years of inflation-induced erosion of their purchasing power. When the White House announced a 7-percent ''voluntary'' limit on wage increases, teachers in communities where lower increases had been offered saw the guidelines as an opportunity to boost demands; elsewhere teachers chose to make larger demands, arguing that they needed to catch up on past lower-than-inflation settlements. For example, teachers in Dayton (Ohio) struck when the board offered an increase of 6.4 to 6.7 percent in response to teacher demands for an increase of 8.5 to 12.4 percent.[42] In Cleveland, where there had been no pay raises for two years, teachers struck in pursuit of their demands for a 20-percent increase.[43] Teachers in Carter County (Tennessee) struck when the board, in an apparent abrogation of a commitment made earlier, approved a budget providing for no increases for teachers.[44] In Collinsville (Illinois) teachers struck after rejecting a proposed salary increase of $500—a raise the teachers construed as having a value of $30 in view of the $470 increase already built into the teachers' salary schedule.[45]

Many school boards believed that they were not in a position to even begin to meet teachers' salary demands. The boards were under increasing financial pressures not merely from inflation-driven increases in the costs of energy and supplies but also from new mandates such as those included in Public Law 94–142—the Education for All Handicapped Children Act—which went into full effect in 1977 and 1978 and which required new spending by local districts. In the state of Washington school-finance-reform efforts imposed lids on spending in wealthy districts, forcing school boards to choose between program cuts and salary increases.[46] In other states the prospect of tax-limitation measures such as California's Proposition 13 spurred some boards to husband their financial resources, just as it spurred some teacher organizations to make salary gains before limitation measures went into effect.

Working conditions for teachers further contributed to the potential for strikes. Violence in the schools had become an occupational hazard. Teacher stress and ''burn-out'' were being widely discussed, along with increasing rates of attrition among experienced teachers. Teachers felt that many of the problems that they were being asked to solve arose in the home and the larger society; the effects of television, broken homes, and poverty could not be redressed in classrooms. Further contributing to teacher headaches was the implementation of regulations flowing from new legislation affecting handicapped students; the regulations burdened teachers with more paperwork and with categories of students whose learning problems were unfamiliar and unsettling.

Although dissatisfaction with working conditions rarely was the direct trigger of strikes, it did fuel the emotions needed to sustain strikes precipitated by other issues. The interconnectedness of salary and working conditions was exemplified by the poststrike musings of a big-city teacher-organization president:

> We had a school system that was being murdered. We had children who were not being educated. We had no plan to regain the state's top-level rating. We teachers are the people who screamed and said, "Our children deserve better than what they're getting." We know that the things that are desirable for children will upgrade our working conditions, and these are the things we're concerned about. Most of all, it's frustrating to care about teaching and to have built-in failure for all of your efforts. . . . You put up with overcrowded conditions and get, maybe in January, supplies that you needed in September. Teachers go to stores and buy things to make their rooms pretty, when actually money has been there [in the system] to do it. Nobody cared enough for us to make it possible for us to do. The human things that are done by teachers for children would astound you. Our people know this. Teachers are interacting with the human lives of children every day. And then to have [management] say those insulting things about people! We should be supported by them. Maybe [management] is so ignorant because they didn't care enough to find out what was going on, or they knew and just simply didn't care. Either way it was hurtful to our people. . . . Anybody who can, gets a job somewhere else without having to put up with the types of problems that we have. Now the board knows that. The superintendent knows it. But they weren't proposing anything that would make it attractive to get people to come in and stay in the system and become professionals. They proposed no improvement in the conditions for professional teachers or for the profession itself. We saw what was happening to our profession. We know that we were all hurting. And we still are in terms of not making adequate salaries. We have gotten further and further behind. Do you know that we used to be on equity with policemen? Now we are behind them. . . . I think it is so sad that our superintendent—who certainly is being treated right about money—never seemed to take the position that for us to really have true professionals in this city, we have to pay people so that they can concentrate on the job of teaching. I would hazard the guess that out of five teachers, three of them moonlight, by necessity. Something is wrong. I don't feel flattered, I feel enraged when a high school kid leaves my class and walks in the next year making as much as I, after I've been teaching twenty-six years. You see something is wrong there. Do you know something? When I sat there on that stage at rally after rally during the strike, people looked happier than they had ever looked. They were taking a stand against all of the things that frustrated them every day.[47]

The comments encapsulate the sentiments and motives of large numbers of teachers who participated in strikes in 1978–1979.

The school managers on whom teachers' spokespersons focused their wrath had grievances of their own. Test scores were falling. There was excessive teacher absenteeism, particularly on Mondays and Fridays. Teachers were booting troublemakers out of classes rather than dealing with them directly. Teachers were resisting the idea of merit pay and objecting to the principle of tying merit to measures of student learning. In the eyes of some boards, it was time to "take a stand" against teachers and to "win back" some of the prerogatives that teachers had won in earlier contracts. In Washington, D.C., for example, salaries were not at issue; when a deadline for contract renewal expired, the board made demands for an increase in the work day and work year.[48] Teachers in Everett, Washington, struck over what they perceived to be contract-stripping efforts by the school board.[49]

Disputes between teachers and school boards were nourished, in part, by interest-mobilization activities conducted by organizations on both sides. On the teachers' side, both the NEA and the AFT were recruiting members. Both organizations had reported membership losses in 1977. Organizing activity was particularly aggressive in the South and the Southwest; most states in that region had yet to adopt statutes permitting bargaining, and both the NEA and the AFT sought to position themselves favorably to capitalize on any bargaining opportunities that might develop.[50] In New Orleans a merged NEA–AFT unit voted to disaffiliate from the NEA in 1977; a strike in 1978 helped to solidify the AFT victory and to establish an AFT stronghold in the deep South.[51] A strike by the NEA unit in East Baton Rouge parish was prompted by the NEA's desire to counter the AFT's gains in New Orleans.[52] A long strike by the AFT local in Saint Louis may have reflected the fact that the Kansas City (Missouri) AFT local had fared badly in a strike the previous year, leaving the AFT in an exposed position in Missouri. In some setting then, the interests at stake extended beyond those of the individual members of the local unit; resources from state and national organizations were concentrated in sites where success or failure in a strike could have extensive consequences for organization membership elsewhere.

As the major teacher organizations sought membership and relative advantage vis-à-vis collective bargaining, management groups were showing growing sophistication in their responses. The National School Boards Association formed the Council of School Board Negotiators; at its first meeting in April 1978 the new Council heard from prominent and experienced representatives of management in bargaining.[53] State school-board associations were employing additional specialists who dispensed training, advice, and direct service to local school boards in matters pertaining to negotiations and strike management. During 1978 a consortium of school-management groups designed a nationwide resource to help school managers deal with teacher power and collective bargaining; the National School Labor Relations Service was launched in early 1979.[54] In more and more communities then, there was growing management resolve and expertise to take a strike if necessary, and to win it.

In the districts where bargaining occurred, it proceeded with varying degrees of sophistication and skill. Some strikes appear to have been triggered by negotiating errors. For example, in Warren (Ohio), teachers struck after the school board failed to ratify a contract agreed to by its own negotiating team.[55] In some communities school boards and even the teachers' own leaders may have underestimated the teachers' determination to gain substantial salary improvement. In Seattle, for example, the teachers' rejection of the board's last-minute offers appears to have startled both sides.[56] Saint Louis teachers surprised their own leaders by voting to reject the board's offers; the third rejection precipitated an eight-week strike at midyear.[57] In some communities the legal and political context for bargaining was so complex and volatile that negotiations were hampered. For example, in Daly City (California), negotiations foundered, in part, over uncertainties about the precise financial implications of Proposition 13 and subsequent state "bail-out" funds.[58] In Cleveland, board negotiators faced the dilemma of finding funds for court-ordered desegration, for complying with state requirements to end deficit spending, and for responding to teacher demands for substantial salary increases.[59] Teacher negotiators also had difficult choices to make as they tried to assure that monetary gains were used to improve salaries, protect jobs, and improve working conditions. Under the circumstances it is perhaps less surprising that bargaining occasionally collapsed than that it so often resulted in settlements.

A few 1978–1979 strikes had their origins in nonbargaining disputes. For example, teachers at a junior high school in University Heights (Ohio) staged a one-day walkout to protest the school administration's failure to expel a student who allegedly assaulted a teacher.[60] In Evanston (Illinois), teachers struck in protest over school-board proposals to cut programs.[61] Such strikes invariably were limited in scope and duration and served primarily to dramatize teachers' concerns rather than to bring pressure to bear on behalf of contractual or bargaining issues.

Whatever their origins, the strikes dramatically altered the teacher-board dispute. New actors became involved—rank-and-file teachers, parents, pickets, reporters, middle managers, civic officials, and community pressure groups. In many instances school boards sought to stop the strikes by seeking injunctive relief.

Notes

1. *Digest of Education Statistics 1980* (Washington, D.C.: National Center for Education Statistics, U.S. Department of Education, 1980), table 7:11 and table 56:60.

2. Roald F. Campbell, Luvern L. Cunningham, and Roderick F. McPhee, *The Organization and Control of American Schools* (Columbus: Merrill, 1965), ch. 10; Edgar B. Wesley, *NEA: The First Hundred Years* (New York: Harper and Row, 1957); and Laurence Iannaccone, *Politics in Education* (New York: Center for Applied Research in Education, 1967).

3. Stephen K. Bailey, Richard T. Frost, Paul E. Marsh, and Robert C. Wood, *Schoolmen and Politics* (Syracuse: Syracuse University Press, 1962); and Iannaccone, *Politics in Education*.

4. Myron Lieberman and Michael H. Moskow, *Collective Negotiations for Teachers* (Chicago: Rand McNally, 1966), ch. 10.

5. Bernard Yabroff and Lily Mary David, "Collective Bargaining and Work Stoppages Involving Teachers," *Monthly Labor Review* 76 (May 1953):478.

6. Data for 1951–1960 from Ronald W. Glass, "Work Stoppages and Teachers: History and Prospect," *Monthly Labor Review* 90 (August 1967):443–446. Data for 1961–1970 from "Teacher Strikes and Work Stoppages," Research Memos #1969–27, #1970–19, and #1971–28 (Washington, D.C.: Research Division, National Education Association). Data for 1971–1979 from "Work Stoppages in Government" published annually by the Bureau of Labor Statistics, U.S. Department of Labor, Washington, D.C.

7. See Glass, "Work Stoppages and Teachers." See also Joseph H. Goergen and John H. Keough, "Issues and Outcomes of Teachers' Strikes, 1955–65" (Ph.D. dissertation, St. John's University, 1967); and Samuel P. Sentelle, "Teacher Strikes in the Public Schools of the United States in 1966" (Ph.D. dissertation, University of Tennessee, 1969).

8. For example, see "Work Stoppages in Government, 1979" (Washington, D.C.: Bureau of Labor Statistics, U.S. Department of Labor, 1981), p. 20.

9. For an excellent summary of this literature, see Anthony M. Cresswell and Michael J. Murphy, *Teachers, Unions, and Collective Bargaining in Education* (Berkeley, Calif.: McCutchan Publishing, 1980), chs. 3 and 4.

10. *Teachers for Tomorrow* (New York: Fund for the Advancement of Education, 1955). See also "Economic Status of Teachers," Research Report 1959–R3 (Washington, D.C.: Research Division, National Education Association, 1959).

11. *Digest,* table 52:57.

12. *The Condition of Education,* 1980 ed. (Washington, D.C.: National Center for Education Statistics, U.S. Department of Education, 1980), p. 76.

13. Raymond Callahan, *Education and the Cult of Efficiency* (Chicago: University of Chicago Press, 1962).

14. Derived from *Digest,* table 55:60.

15. Chris Argyris, *Personality and Organization* (New York: Harper and Row, 1957); and Francis M. Trusty, ed., *Administering Human Resources* (Berkeley, Calif.: McCutchan Publishing, 1971).

16. John Holt, *How Children Fail* (New York: Delta, 1964); Jonathan Kozol, *Death at an Early Age: The Destruction of the Hearts and Minds of Negro Children in the Boston Public Schools* (Boston: Houghton Mifflin, 1967); James Herndon, *The Way It Spozed to Be: A Report on the Classroom War Behind the Crisis in Our Schools* (New York: Simon & Schuster, 1968); and Bel Kaufman, *Up the Down Staircase* (Englewood Cliffs, N.J.: Prentice-Hall, 1964).

17. Dan C. Lortie, *Schoolteacher* (Chicago: University of Chicago Press, 1975), ch. 7.

18. Ronald Corwin, "Professional Persons in Public Organizations," *Educational Administration Quarterly* 1 (Autumn 1965):1–22.

19. "School Boards in an Era of Conflict: Highlights of the Cubberley Conference, Stanford University, July 26–28, 1966" (Washington, D.C.: National School Public Relations Association, n.d.).

20. For example, see Robert Bendiner, *The Politics of Schools: A Crisis in Self-Government* (New York: Harper and Row, 1969). See also Michael D. Usdan, "The Future Viability of the School Board," ed. Peter J. Cistone, *Understanding School Boards* (Lexington, Mass.: D.C. Heath, 1975), ch. 14.

21. Myron Lieberman, "Teachers' Strikes: An Analysis of the Issues," *Harvard Educational Review* 26 (Winter 1956):67.

22. Myron Lieberman, *Education as a Profession* (Englewood Cliffs, N.J.: Prentice-Hall, 1956); and Myron Lieberman, *The Future of Public Education* (Chicago: University of Chicago Press, 1960).

23. Richard A. Schmuck and Matthew B. Miles, eds., *Organization Development in Schools* (Palo Alto, Calif.: National Press Books, 1971).

24. For accounts of the New York City strike, see Alan Rosenthal, *Pedagogues and Power: Teacher Groups in School Politics* (Syracuse: Syracuse University Press, 1969); and Stephen Cole, *The Unionization of Teachers: A Case Study of the UFT* (New York: Praeger, 1969).

25. For example, see Ellen Hogan Steele, "II: A Teacher's View," *Phi Delta Kappan* 57 (May 1976):590–592.

26. Lieberman and Moskow, *Collective Negotiations,* pp. 303–309.

27. *Government Employee Relations Report RF 152* (Washington, D.C.: Bureau of National Affairs, November 21, 77) 41:101–130.

28. Randal A. Lemke, "An Analysis of the Saint Louis Teachers' Strike: January to March, 1979" (Ph.D. dissertation, Washington University, Saint Louis, 1980), pp. 18–27.

29. *National League of Cities v. Usery,* 426 U.S. 833 (1976).

30. *Hortonville Joint School District No. 1 v. Hortonville Education Association,* 426 U.S. 482 (1976).

31. *Commonwealth of Virginia v. The County Board of Education of Arlington County,* Va. Sup. Ct., 232 S.E.2d. 30 (1977).

32. *St. Louis Teachers Association v. Board of Education of St. Louis,* Mo. Sup. Ct., 544 S.W.2d. 573 (1976).

33. Phil Ward, "Why Our Strike Failed," *Learning* (April 1980):30–33.

34. For example, see American Association of School Administrators, "Work Stoppage Strategies," Executive Handbook Series, #6 (Washington, D.C.: American Association of School Administrators, 1975); Max A. Bailey and Ronald R. Booth, "Collective Bargaining and the School Board Member" (Springfield, Ill.: Illinois Association of School Boards, 1978); and Association of California School Administrators, *Strike Manual* (Burlingame, Calif.: Association of California School Administrators, 1973).

35. Anthony Cresswell and Daniel Simpson, "Collective Bargaining and Conflict: Impacts on School Governance," *Educational Administration Quarterly* 13 (Fall 1977):49–69.

36. Bendiner, *Politics of Schools,* p. 118.

37. Douglas E. Mitchell, Charles T. Kerchner, Wayne Erck, and Gabrielle Pryor, "The Impact of Collective Bargaining on School Management and Policy," *American Journal of Education* 89 (February 1981):147–188.

38. Lorraine McDonnell and Anthony Pascal, "Organized Teachers in American Schools" (Santa Monica, Calif.: Rand, R–2407–NIE, 1979).

39. Ida Klaus, "The Evolution of a Collective Bargaining Relationship in Public Education: New York City's Changing Seven-Year History," *Michigan Law Review* 67 (1969):1033–1066.

40. Martin Mayer, *The Teachers Strike: New York 1968* (New York: Harper and Row, 1968); Melvin I. Urofsky, *Why Teachers Strike: Teachers' Rights and Community Control* (Garden City, N.J.: Anchor-Doubleday, 1970); and Barbara Carter, *Pickets, Parents, and Power* (New York: Citation, 1971).

41. Edith E. Graber, "Survey of 1978–1979 Teacher Strikes," mimeographed (Saint Louis: Center for the Study of Law in Education, Washington University, 1980).

42. *Government Employee Relations Report* (Washington, D.C.: Bureau of National Affairs, October 9, 1978) 780:18.

43. *Cleveland Plain Dealer,* August 31, 1981.

44. *Memphis Commercial Appeal,* January 8, 1979.

45. David L. Colton, "A Teacher Strike in Collinsville, Illinois," mimeographed (Saint Louis: Center for the Study of Law in Education, Washington University, 1980).

46. David L. Colton, "State of Washington: Four Courts," mimeographed (Saint Louis: Center for the Study of Law in Education, Washington University, 1980).

47. To protect confidentiality, interview sources are not identified in this book.

48. *Washington Star,* March 6, 1979.

49. Colton, "State of Washington."

50. *Government Employee Relations Report RF 184* (Washington, D.C.: Bureau of National Affairs, November 26, 1979) 41:305–348.

51. *Government Employee Relations Report* (Washington, D.C.: Bureau of National Affairs, September 25, 1978) 778:17.

52. Ward, "Why Our Strike Failed."

53. *Government Employee Relations Report* (Washington, D.C.: Bureau of National Affairs, April 10, 1978) 754:17.

54. See "NSLRS: Practical Resources for School Labor Relations," *NSLRS* (Washington, D.C.: National School Labor Relations Service), vol. 1, no. 1 (September 1979).

55. *Columbus Citizen-Journal,* August 29, 1978.

56. Colton, "State of Washington."

57. Lemke, "An Analysis of the St. Louis Teachers' Strike," pp. 135–137.

58. Edith E. Graber, "California: The Daly City Strike," mimeographed (Saint Louis: Center for the Study of Law in Education, Washington University, 1980).

59. *Cleveland Plain Dealer,* September 17, 1978.

60. *Cleveland Plain Dealer,* March 24, 1979.

61. *Chicago Sun Times,* April 5, 1979.

3 The Legal Dispute

Courts are dispute-processing institutions for society. But social disputes cannot be taken to court in their raw form. Courts can deal only with legal disputes. Because there is nothing illegal about it, an impasse in the teacher-bargaining process does not present an occasion for going to court. A strike does. A strike transforms the bargaining dispute by creating a pretext for asking a legal question: Should the strike be enjoined? School-board petitioners can claim that a teacher strike is illegal, that it impedes the petitioners' capacity to perform their legally required duty to operate schools, and that the teachers therefore ought to be ordered to cease their strike.

However, teachers are using the strike as a bargaining tactic to achieve a favorable disposition of the issues in dispute at the bargaining table: If they are required to give up their strike, they will be at a power disadvantage for they will have lost the power of noncooperation. Thus teacher defendants in an injunction proceeding normally use every legal means to delay, deflect, or prevent the issuance of an injunction and to turn the proceedings to their own advantage if possible.

Once in court, board petitioners and teacher defendants have to process their legal dispute in terms of the substantive and procedural requirements of the legal system. Bargaining-table issues and tactics no longer apply. Statutes, previous cases, and judicial rules of procedure provide the standards that are employed to ascertain the court's jurisdiction over parties and issues, the points of law that are disputed, the types of evidence that may be utilized, and the bases for ultimate judicial decision.

When a social dispute is transferred to court, there is also a change in personnel. Negotiating teams, public-relations officers, and union and board officials are the chief actors in the bargaining-table dispute. Attorneys for both sides, if involved at all, normally occupy a marginal, sideline role. However, when the dispute moves to court, the leading roles fall to members of the legal profession. Attorneys and judges become chief actors both in shaping issues and in resolving them.

The Injunctive Process

An injunction is a court order commanding a person or persons to refrain from doing some act (for example, building a dam, discriminating against women, or engaging in a strike). Or persons may be required to perform some positive act.[1] If the person so commanded disobeys, the judge can find the party in contempt of court and impose fines or a jail sentence or both. The judge can thus, by a court order, alter the balance of power and advantage between the parties and dramatically affect the outcome of the dispute.

Injunctions originated in English courts. They were created to deal with situations in which some action would, if permitted to occur or to continue, be both unjust and noncompensable. Faced with such situations, potential victims could seek an injunction barring the act.

Injunction proceedings place extraordinary powers in the hands of judges. In contrast to judicial proceedings arising from events that have already occurred, injunction proceedings often deal with *prospective* events where both the likelihood of occurrence and the nature of the consequences are conjectural. Judgments made in such a manner permit and require the exercise of great discretion. Additional discretionary judgment is required in situations where the legality of the threatened action is in dispute—as is often the case with teacher strikes.

The injunctive process also gives courts great powers to sanction. The party disobeying a court order may be charged with either civil or criminal contempt. The charge of civil contempt is applied to acts that appear to be directed not to the dignity of the court but to the rights and claims of the petitioners in whose interests the court order was issued. Sanctions are remedial; when parties comply, the penalty ceases. The charge of criminal contempt, however, is applied to acts that are interpreted as challenging the dignity and authority of the court and obstructing its work. Sanctions are punitive and may be levied against defiant parties whether or not they subsequently comply. The court itself may initiate the criminal-contempt action.[2] It may also bring the action even though the employer prefers that contempt charges be dismissed.

Respondents are, in general, legally required to obey the injunction even though they charge that there were errors in the trial-court proceeding. In numerous contempt cases, parties have been advised that if they do not like the law, they should turn to the legislature; if they do not like the injunction, they may appeal to a higher court. In the meantime they must abide by the order.

Clearly, there are opportunities for injustice here. Parties seeking injunctive relief may, and often do, wait until the last possible moment before going to court, thus strengthening their ability to convince the court that the threatened action is imminent or has already begun to occur and that it is not merely conjectural. But if it is imminent, the court may be requested to act quickly. Hence, there is no opportunity for the normal adversary process to work. Actions may be enjoined on an *ex parte* basis, that is, without notice or an opportunity for the party being charged to be present or represented. Thus a judge's own values and views—normally constrained by the adversary process—may come into play. In contempt proceedings where the court itself is the aggrieved party, dispassionate justice may be less likely than it is in situations where the court itself has no stakes in the dispute or its outcomes.

Over the centuries, efforts to constrain the possibilities of judicial abuse of injunctive powers have taken a number of forms, which together constitute the framework for injunction proceedings today. Usually the constraints are not codified; rather, they take the form of maxims and precepts of equity that are to be applied by the judge to the situation at hand. One is that *ex parte* injunctions (those granted without a two-party hearing) are of limited duration. Typically they last for only a few days until there has been a "show cause" hearing at which the enjoined party has an opportunity to present arguments showing why the injunction should be lifted. If those arguments do not prevail, a preliminary injunction may be issued. It too is of limited duration. Because of its serious nature, a permanent injunction may not be issued until a full hearing has been held. Once issued, it remains in effect until altered by the court.

There are other standards governing the availability of injunctive relief. One is that the act must threaten more than mere inconvenience; it must threaten *irreparable harm*. The party seeking relief must have *clean hands,* that is, must not have precipitated the threatened actions by his or her own deeds. The petitioner must persuade the court that there is *no adequate remedy at law,* that is, that an injunction is the only reasonable form of relief available. There must be a *balancing of the equities,* that is, a judgement that the harm wrought upon the party enjoined is less than the harm that the petitioner seeks to prevent. Finally, injunctions are not to be issued if they cannot be enforced.

It is up to the court to apply these standards. Thus the court must not only ascertain their meanings but must also weigh their relative significance in a particular situation. And all of this often must be done, it will be recalled, without benefit of the full-blown adversarial proceeding that normally is designed to present to the court a full range of facts and a careful examination of the law. In *ex parte* proceedings, only one perspective is heard. In preliminary injunction proceedings, the adversary process is often truncated, again presenting a less-than-complete view of the situation.

In fashioning their responses to requests for injunctive relief, judges have a great deal of latitude. The judge may entirely accept the petitioners' arguments and grant the relief requested. The judge may accept some contentions, reject others, and grant partial relief. The court may attempt to fashion a remedy that protects the interests of both parties. Or the court may refuse to act at all, dismissing the case or delaying proceedings to such an extent that the parties are effectively left to their own devices. Whatever the judge does, however, must be justified in terms of established traditions of injunction proceedings. The manner in which these arguments are presented to the judge and the manner in which the judge deals with them are the essence of the injunctive process.

Some commentators contend that the injunction constitutes one of the most significant and useful forms of judicial action. In recent years injunctions have been used to address a host of problems outside the domain of labor-management disputes: school segregation, malapportionment of electoral districts, environmental threats, injustices in prisons and hospitals, and protest movements of various kinds. Civil-rights leaders have devised strategies for capitalizing on civil disobedience of injunctions directed to thwarting efforts to promote social justice.[3]

But among leaders of the labor movement, the injunction is usually seen as a form of harassment. That view has its roots in an era when injunctions were used to oppose unionism, collective bargaining, and strikes.

Use of the Injunction in the Private Sector

In the late nineteenth century, the injunction became a powerful tool used by business interests to prevent or terminate work stoppages. A business faced with a work stoppage would file a complaint alleging that the stoppage would cause irreparable harm to property rights and that only an injunction could prevent such harm. Well-established principles of equity were cited by skilled corporate attorneys to judges sympathetic to property rights. The injunction, if issued, ordered workers to remain at their positions pending a hearing of the case. Failure to comply made the workers and their organizations vulnerable to contempt-of-court proceedings, fines, and jail sentences. The injunction was thus viewed by labor as a strike-breaking tactic. One such case was that of Eugene Debs, leader of the American Railway Union. In 1894 the union engaged in a sympathy strike supporting Pullman workers; their joint work stoppage tied up the railroads of the nation. An injunction was sought and obtained. Federal troops arrested Debs, breaking the strike. In the following year, the U.S. Supreme Court affirmed the action of the lower court.[4] By the

1920s, labor injunctions had become effective and widely used antilabor devices.

Labor leaders asserted that such practices unfairly aligned the coercive powers of government with the interests of management. Courts, they argued, were not maintaining the requisite impartiality and neutrality in private-sector strike cases. Labor directed much of its growing political power to the task of securing legislation that would limit or ban the use of labor injunctions. In 1930 this campaign received a substantial boost in the form of a book coauthored by Harvard law professor Felix Frankfurter and Nathan Greene. Their book, *The Labor Injunction*,[5] documented the development and use of the labor injunction in this country and sharply denounced the abuse of equitable powers by the courts and the acquiescence of legislatures in that abuse. Frankfurter and Greene were especially critical of the denial of due process in the ready use of *ex parte* relief and of the routine way in which courts uncritically accepted plaintiff's claims about the extent and nature of harm. They suggested that such abuses of judicial power constituted a serious threat to the integrity and legitimacy of law and legal institutions of America.

Frankfurter and Greene's book appeared in the the early stages of the Great Depression and helped pave the way for adoption of the Norris-LaGuardia Act in 1932. The act curtailed the use of labor injunctions by federal courts. Many states soon followed with "Little Norris-LaGuardia Acts," which sought to restrict the use of labor injunctions in private-sector disputes before state courts. These acts signaled the end of the era of "government by injunction" in private-sector labor relations. They paved the way for later New Deal legislation regularizing the collective-bargaining process and formally recognizing the right to strike.

The Use of Injunctions in the Public Sector

In the middle third of this century teachers and other federal, state, and local government employees watched as industrial and craft workers gained income, security, and a voice in working conditions through collective bargaining and occasional strikes. But these avenues of assertion were closed to public employees, for in the absence of legislative or executive or judicial authorization, employers had no right to engage in bargaining and employees had no right to strike. When public-sector employees argued that the labor legislation of the 1930s applied to public workers, they often found the courts unsympathetic. For example, in *United States* v. *United Mine Workers*,[6] the U.S. Supreme Court held that the Norris-LaGuardia Act did not apply to public-sector strikes at the federal level. However, legislatures and executive agencies, aware that by midcentury, public employees constituted one-fifth of the work force, proved to be more receptive. Major breakthroughs authorizing public-employee bargaining came with the passage of Wisconsin's public-employee bargaining law in 1959 and President Kennedy's 1961 executive order encouraging collective organization among federal employees. In subsequent years bargaining statutes became widespread. By 1980, thirty-one states had statutes that authorized or required some form of teacher–board collective relationships (see appendix). In many other states bargaining-like activities occur even in the absence of statutory authorization.

Public employees have made relatively little progress in obtaining a right to strike. By 1980 only seven states (Alaska, Hawaii, Minnesota, Oregon, Pennsylvania, Wisconsin, and Vermont) had given teachers such a statutory right. Even in these states the right is severely circumscribed. Most of these states created a time frame within which strikes may be countenanced: A teacher strike is legal only if certain preconditions are met, and it remains legal only as long as certain consequences are avoided. In the remaining forty-three states there is no statutory right to strike for teachers. Indeed, in twenty-two of these states teacher strikes are expressly prohibited by statute. In the remaining twenty-one states the statutes are silent on the matter of teacher strikes.

Frustrated in their efforts to obtain legislative approval of strikes, teachers have turned to the courts for support. Constitutional arguments have been advanced; teacher attorneys have contended that bans on strikes violated First Amendment freedoms of speech, expression, and assembly; Thirteenth Amendment prohibitions against involuntary servitude; and Fourteenth Amendment assurances of equal protection. Such arguments have been uniformly rejected by the courts.

Teachers have been similarly unsuccessful in establishing a common-law basis for strikes. In a 1951 Connecticut case the Norwalk Teachers' Association applied to the court for a declaratory judgment asking, among other matters, whether teachers could engage in a strike. The state's high court replied:

> Under our system, the government is established by and run for all of the people, not for the benefit of any person or group. The profit motive, inherent in the principle of free enterprise, is absent. It should be the aim of every employee of the government to do his or her part to make it function as efficiently and economically as possible. The drastic remedy of the organized strike to enforce the demands of government employees is in direct contravention of this principle. . . . [Government employees] occupy a status entirely different from those who carry on a private enterprise. They serve the public welfare and not a private purpose. To say that they can strike is the equivalent of saying that they

can deny the authority of government and contravene the public welfare.[7]

The court then went on to enunciate a position that today remains a central tenet of court adjudication of teacher strikes:

Few cases involving the right of unions of government employees to strike to enforce their demands have reached courts of last resort. That right has usually been tested by an application for an injunction forbidding the strike. The right of the governmental body to this relief has been uniformly upheld.[8]

In a 1957 case, a New Hampshire court refused to obliterate the distinction between private- and public-sector strikes. The court acknowledged that a strike by teachers had been "conducted in a completely peaceful manner, without violence, picket lines, disturbances or damage to person or property." The court continued:

Any modification in the common law doctrine that the sovereignty of the state should not be hampered by strikes by public employees involves a change in public policy. It has been the consistent opinion of this court that such a change is for the Legislature to determine rather than being within the province of the court.[9]

In 1958 the supreme court of Rhode Island addressed the applicability of anti-injunction legislation to public-sector cases. It concluded, "The abuses which anti-injunction legislation was aimed at correcting did not involve labor disputes between the government, national, state or local, and its employees."[10] Noting that "the determination of the present issue depends upon the basic difference between governmental employment and employment in private industry," the court found that the teachers on strike were "agents of the state government and as such exercise a portion of the sovereign power." Absent a clear statutory declaration by the state legislature that granted a right to strike, teachers had "no right to strike against the government."[11] In these and a host of similar cases, the courts outlined their principal position on teacher strikes: Absent legislative authorization, such strikes were illegal and hence enjoinable. If legislatures have been chary of granting teachers a right to strike, the courts have been even more so.

However, there has been one crack in the otherwise formidable wall of support for issuance of injunctive relief in the face of strikes. Because injunctions are such powerful weapons, the courts have gradually evolved restrictions on their use, even in the face of clearly illegal actions. A 1968 case, *Holland School District* v. *Holland Education Association,* made these restrictions significant for teachers.[12] In 1965 Michigan had become one of the first states to adopt a statute authorizing teacher–board bargaining. The statute banned strikes, but it was silent as to the availability of injunctive relief in the face of an illegal strike. An injunction issued in connection with a teacher strike in the city of Holland reached the state's supreme court. That body affirmed the power of the courts to enjoin strikes by public employees. However, it held that the fact that an injunction *could* issue did not necessarily mean that it *must* issue, for that would "destroy the independence of the judicial branch of government." The illegality of the strike was not, in itself, sufficient grounds for an injunction. The court then turned to the question of "whether . . . the chancellor [the judge in the lower court who had enjoined the strike] had before him that quantum of proof or uncontradicted allegations of fact which would justify the issuance of an injunction in a labor dispute." The court found that he had not:

> We here hold it is insufficient merely to show that a concert of prohibited action by public employees has taken place and that *ipso facto* such a showing justifies injunctive relief. We so hold because it is basically contrary to public policy in this State to issue injunctions in labor disputes absent a showing of violence, irreparable injury, or breach of the peace. . . . Simply put, the only showing made to the chancellor was that if an injunction did not issue, the district's schools would not open, staffed by teachers on the date scheduled for such opening. We hold such showing insufficient to have justified the exercise of the plenary power of equity by the force of injunction.[13]

While the court failed to specify what would constitute the necessary "quantum of proof," it did suggest that on remand the lower court consider whether "the plaintiff school district has refused to bargain in good faith, whether an injunction should issue at all, and if so, on what terms and for what period in light of the whole record to be adduced." With these words, the court affirmed the principle of judicial discretion in injunction cases. Later we shall see how teachers have capitalized on the opportunity created by *Holland* and its progeny.

The progeny are few in number.[14] In the 1973 *Westerly* case, the Rhode Island Supreme Court, after affirming earlier holdings that teachers did not have the right to strike in the absence of legislative authorization and that the courts could enjoin strikes, observed that it did not follow that "every time there is a concerted work stoppage by public employees, it shall be subject to an automatic restraining order." The court took note of the state Rules of Civil Procedure, which specified,

> No temporary restraining order shall be granted without notice to the adverse party unless it clearly appears from specific facts by affidavit

or verified complaint that irreparable harm will result before notice can
be served and a hearing held.[15]

The court acknowledged that the plaintiffs had filed a general affidavit
averring that the schools could not open as scheduled and that irreparable
harm would ensue. But, said the court,

> The mere failure of a public school system to begin its school year on
> the appointed day cannot be classified as a catastrophic event. We are
> . . . aware that there has been no public furor when schools are closed
> because of inclement weather, or on the day a presidential candidate
> comes to town, or when the basketball team wins the championship.
> The law requires that the schools be in session for 180 days a year. . . .
> There is a flexibility in the calendaring of the school year that not only
> permits the makeup of days which might have been missed for one
> reason or another but may also negate the necessity of the immediate
> injunction which could conceivably subject some individuals to the
> court's plenary power of contempt.[16]

Thus the court found the evidence insufficient to warrant a temporary
restraining order. The order was quashed.

In 1974 the New Hampshire Supreme Court took up the *Holland*
banner in *Timberlane Regional School District* v. *Timberlane Regional
Education Association*. Reviewing (and upholding) a lower court's refusal
to issue an injunction against striking teachers, the court noted,

> The injunction is an extraordinary remedy which is only granted under
> circumstances where a plaintiff has no adequate remedy at law and is
> likely to suffer irreparable harm unless the conduct of the defendant is
> enjoined. The availability of injunctive relief is a matter within the
> sound discretion of the court, exercised on a consideration of all the
> circumstances of each case and controlled by established principles of
> equity.[17]

Citing *Holland* and *Westerly,* the court stated,

> Accordingly, it is our view that in deciding to withhold an injunction
> the trial court may properly consider among other factors whether rec-
> ognized methods of settlement have failed, whether negotiations have
> been conducted in good faith, and whether the public health, safety and
> welfare will be substantially harmed if the strike is allowed to continue.[18]

Later decisions in Wisconsin and Idaho also incorporated the *Holland*
restraints on the issuance of injunctive relief.[19] Such decisions have been
rare. In the vast majority of cases courts have held to the *Norwalk* position
rather than to the holding in *Holland*.

Boards usually choose to argue the *Norwalk* line of precedents that absent a legal right to strike, teacher strikes should be enjoined. Teachers, however, have found in *Holland* a useful defense against injunctions. By attempting to focus the attention of the court on the propriety of issuing injunctive relief, rather than on the question of the legality of the strike, and by capitalizing on the procedural opportunities inherent in legal proceedings, teacher attorneys have been able to delay and confound injunction proceedings in ways that enhance their clients' interests. These tactics also pose major problems for judicial disposition.

The Injunctive Process in the Center City School Strike

The following account of the teacher-strike injunctive process is a composite of our on-site studies of strikes in nine states in 1978–1979 and of media and participants' accounts of strikes in other states. No known injunction proceeding incorporates all the elements portrayed here. Details were selected to illustrate some of the issues that arise in teacher-strike processing in court.

The hypothetical strike described here took place in a state in which statutory law prohibits teacher strikes and specifies that when they occur, they may be enjoined. However, a recent state appellate court decision held that principles of equity—the need to show harm, the requirement that the board come to court with clean hands, the holding of show cause hearings except in situations of dire emergency—should be followed carefully before an injunction is issued.

Tuesday, September 6: On Tuesday morning, the 1,630 teachers and professional employees of the Center City School District went on strike. Teachers had been without a contract for the previous six months but had continued teaching while the board extended the previous contract.

Monday, September 12: Attorneys for the board announced that they would file a complaint for injunctive relief on Wednesday if the dispute were not settled by then. School administrators indicated that they had not sought an injunction during the first week of the strike since some recent teacher cases in state courts had been denied immediate relief. However, they cited to reporters the "growing pressures from countless parents who, because of the strike, have to sit at home or arrange child care so they can continue their jobs."

An assistant superintendent indicated that if the strike were to last beyond September 19, it would be necessary to teach on holidays and during summer vacation in order to complete the legally required 180 days of instruction.

Wednesday, September 14: Board attorneys filed with the Center

County Civil Court a complaint requesting both an *ex parte* temporary restraining order and a preliminary injunction. Judge John Davis denied the temporary restraining order, citing recent appellate cases and noting that there had been no demonstration of a true emergency. He set a show cause hearing for Monday, September 19, at 10:00 a.m. He did order some restrictions on picketing. And he ordered the parties to negotiate for a minimum of four hours a day until the Monday hearing.

Also on September 14, board attorneys filed with the court a "Complaint in Equity." They argued that teacher strikes were prohibited by statute in the state, that a number of appellate cases had upheld that prohibition, and that striking teachers should be enjoined. The complaint also cited what a teacher attorney called "a normal litany of harm." It stated that the strike was causing and would continue to cause irreparable harm to the educational program of the district, to the continuity of instruction to students (and especially to special programs for the handicapped); it would constitute a threat to the provision of 180 days of instruction and thereby result in the loss of state and federal subsidy; it would cause hardships for graduating seniors if classes were extended into the summer (thereby disrupting summer entrance to college or the armed forces and delaying the transmission of final grades for college entrance); it would deprive needy students of the daily lunch program; and it would cause the cessation of community educational programs. Plaintiffs asserted that there was no adequate remedy at law, and therefore they requested a preliminary injunction that would order teachers to cease striking.

Board attorneys also filed affidavits from the board president, the superintendent, and the associate superintendent for instruction further characterizing the harm being caused by the strike. One noted the "hundreds of complaints, statements of concern, and pleas from citizens, parents, and students to open schools." It cited the "harmful impression left upon thousands of young citizens, the district's students, by their teachers striking in disregard of state law and contractual requirements." Another noted that make-up days would substantially increase maintenance and personnel costs for the district.

In addition, administrative officials quoted from letters from the state department of education asserting that students had a primary right to receive 180 days of instruction and that districts "will be encouraged to seek court injunctions against any strike which will make that impossible."

Teacher attorneys filed a document entitled "Answer and New Matter" with the court before the show cause hearing. They denied that the district was unable to provide an educational program; they held that the program was only delayed, not denied. The strike was not causing harm to the educational program since the school calendar could be rescheduled. Defendants argued that the points raised by the board asserting the existence of harm were "conclusory allegations" and they demanded "strict proof" of the allegations at the time of the hearing.

In "New Matter," defendants brought countercharges against the board, seeking to introduce some of the issues in the bargaining-table dispute. They charged that the work stoppage was not a strike but a lockout since the board had refused to extend all the terms and conditions of the expired contract and had thus "changed the status quo." Further, the document asserted that plaintiff was guilty of unclean hands by failing to state that if the injunction were obtained, the board would reschedule the requisite days of instruction.

Defendants also filed a "Motion for Summary and/or Accelerated Judgment" contending that the suit should be dismissed since (1) the meeting at which the board had decided to seek an injunction had not been held in compliance with the state's "open meetings law" and the action taken was therefore not in keeping with law; (2) since no contract existed between the parties, there was no obligation to work; (3) the current strike case was pending before the Public Employee Relations Board, and therefore, court action was premature; and (4) the board had not exhausted its administrative remedies (firing and other administrative sanctions). Therefore, the case was improperly before the court.

Board attorneys filed a reply to the "New Matter," requesting that it be struck since matters set forth there were irrelevant to issues raised in the "Complaint." The issue before the court was the illegal strike. All else was not germane. The board stated that teachers were refusing to work; in view of this, plaintiff was under no obligation to implement the expired contract. Further, alternative scheduling was a "speculative" matter, subject to approval by the state department of education. Finally, plaintiff denied "unclean hands."

Board attorneys also filed a "Memorandum of Law" arguing again that both the legislature and the courts had declared public-sector strikes illegal. Attorneys argued that the legislative prohibition indicated a presumption on the part of lawmakers that such strikes were per se harmful. Hence it was not really necessary to demonstrate harm. Nevertheless, the memorandum proceeded to substantiate the existence of harm, adducing additional injury in the cancellation of extracurricular activities, in the example provided to students who saw their teachers breaking the law, in cessation of the district's programs for drop-outs, and in the potential loss of subsidy to the district because students were transferring to nearby districts.

Monday, September 19: The show cause hearing had been set for

10:00 a.m. However, parents and media reporters waited in the courtroom until 2:30 p.m. before Judge John Davis appeared. Judge Davis indicated that an attempt had been made to resolve the dispute in chambers. He had met with both parties and had then conferred separately with a representative of each party. But the attempt to resolve the dispute had been unsuccessful. Hence, the case would proceed. He denied a motion by teacher attorneys to dismiss the case. The first witness for the board was the associate superintendent for finance who testified that the district was incurring extra expenses during the strike because of the need to have support personnel in place and ready for the resumption of schooling. He listed extra energy costs should make-up days require teaching on school holidays or during summer vacation. Under cross-examination, the associate superintendent acknowledged that it would still be possible to secure 180 days of instruction using vacation days if the strike were over before October 13, a date nearly a month away.

The second witness, the associate superintendent for instruction, was asked whether a six-day school week would be a viable option in meeting the 180-day requirement. He felt it would not be, suggesting that the intensity of instruction would yield diminishing returns for efforts exerted. Further, children would be deprived of family time on weekends, time that was beneficial to the learning experience. Extending the school year into the summer would have disadvantageous effects on seniors seeking early admission to college, to summer jobs, or to military service; summer-school sessions would also be jeopardized.

He was asked what effect continuation of the strike would have on student receptivity to the educational process. He testified in answer that he had been driving past one of the high schools and had seen a student carrying a sign "My teacher is a lawbreaker." He interpreted this as an indication of hostility that would impair the positive teacher–student interaction necessary for effective instruction.

On cross-examination, the associate superintendent was asked for specific studies, research findings, or facts that would give evidence that the six-day school week was counterproductive, that time away from parents was harmful to learning outcomes, and that extending the school year would have a detrimental effect on college admissions. The associate superintendent could cite no specific studies but asserted that, given time, he could produce such data. With this, the board concluded its case.

Teacher attorneys made a motion to dismiss on grounds that the plaintiff board had failed to prove its case. Judge Davis denied the motion, indicating that in such a case, he took "the facts plaintiff had elicited from the witness as being true" and that it was arguable that sufficient grounds existed for the issuance of an injunction. The board attorney then requested that the preliminary injunction be granted. But the judge asserted that defendants should be given "their day in court."

Teachers called only one witness. It was Professor Jim Green from the State University Department of Elementary and Secondary Education. Professor Green was asked whether a two- or three-week strike would have an adverse effect on the learning outcomes of children and on their relationship with teachers. He asserted that it need not have such an effect, depending on how the matter was handled by teachers and parents. When asked to document his statement with research findings, he cited a study conducted during a Philadelphia school strike in 1972.[20] Achievement tests had been given before the strike began. The finding was that there was no difference in the rise of achievement levels of children who had been in school and those who had been out during the entire eight weeks. He also referred to studies that indicate that schooling had little measurable impact on student success or failure in life. An absence because of a teacher strike should therefore not affect pupils adversely. (Defendants' attorney later acknowledged that this was a two-edged argument, likely to undercut the position of teachers in some later contention that their work was important to the lives and learning outcomes of children. They were uncomfortable with the argument but used it nonetheless.)

Professor Green was asked whether a six-day week for make-up purposes would cause harm. He replied that, based on evidence in Japan and Europe where Saturday classes were routinely held, it would be difficult to infer harm. As to spacing and length of vacation periods, he testified that the literature was inconclusive as to the optimum duration. As to the learning experience between pupils and teachers, he testified that there was always some anxiety and turmoil in a strike situation. However, the state was a key labor state, and some parents had themselves been involved in strikes. Under those conditions, he found it difficult to conceive that students would be negatively impressed by a teacher who had engaged in collective bargaining and strikes. When asked whether a lengthened school year would jeopardize college admissions, he testified that at State University, allowances were made for such situations.

On cross-examination, he concurred that the cited Philadelphia study was concerned with school achievement, not with student attitudes. He was asked whether he would recommend a seven-day school week; he said he would not. He was then questioned when harm begins to occur. Green noted that test results in the Philadelphia study had indicated that there had been no harm as a result of an eight-week strike.

In summation, the teachers' attorney argued that a case had not been made for irreparable injury and that, in keeping with this, "I don't see how this Court can issue an injunction."

Judge Davis then gave his oral decision. He noted that teachers should not be required to subsidize the community with their low wages. On the other hand, the school board had indicated that there simply was not enough money to give teachers the requested raise, given their responsibility to run a solvent district. He noted that state law held that public employees cannot strike. Such a strike was occurring. The next question was whether irreparable harm existed. Both counsel had addressed themselves to this question. Learned men had testified on both sides, but they were far apart on their assessment of the consequences of the strike and on the existence of harm. The judge was thus left with a battle of the experts. For him, harm was epitomized by the student carrying the sign "My teacher is a lawbreaker." That erosion of relationship seemed to encapsulate, for the judge, a harmful consequence. He also found harm to special-education students who needed continuity of instruction and a sustained learning environment. In addition, he found that there was harm to the board, to teachers themselves, and to the community. The public was being deprived of services for which they were paying. To secure those services, the judge issued a preliminary injunction ordering the teachers to end their strike.

Tuesday, September 20: Teachers met from seven to noon. They decided by a narrow margin to continue the strike, thus defying the order of the court. The Center City school administration announced late in the day that it intended to fire teachers and began to accept applications to replace them. Meanwhile negotiations continued at an undisclosed location.

Thursday, September 22: The board filed with the court a "Petition to Punish for Contempt." A show cause hearing was set for Monday, September 26. The board also fired twenty-four striking teachers.

Monday, September 26: The show cause hearing on the contempt charges was delayed for two hours while parties met with the judge in chambers. The hearing lasted only a few minutes. Judge Davis indicated that because good-faith negotiations were continuing, he would defer a decision on contempt charges. He appointed a "Master of the Court" to represent him in negotiations and to make daily progress reports to the court. He also noted that he would convene the court on short notice and issue contempt citations summarily if he felt such action were justified.

Late Monday night, after the hearing, negotiation continued. A tentative agreement was reached during the night and was ratified by teachers the following afternoon. The agreement included an amnesty clause. All fired teachers who returned to work by Wednesday morning would "not be subject to discipline." All twenty-four fired teachers returned. The strike that lasted fifteen instructional days was over.

In summary, several points may be noted about the Center City School strike. First, the parties used arguments that would further their own goals. The board argued illegality of strike action and the presence of harm as a result of such illegal action. With a court decision in its favor, the board would gain bargaining advantages. When teachers defied court orders to cease striking the board again went to court to seek a favorable decision for themselves and one that would put added pressure on teachers. When Judge Davis refused to act on the charges, the board was denied such legal backing. In the words of a teacher source, "That night was when the real bargaining began and we soon came to agreement."

Teachers sought to have the action dismissed on a variety of grounds and then argued that the board had not proven its case. When those actions failed, they argued that a teacher strike did not cause harm and that, even if it did, the harm was not irreparable since lost days could be rescheduled. That argument too failed. Teachers also sought to introduce bargaining-table issues into the court confrontation at several points, charging that the board was guilty of unclean hands and unfair bargaining, again without sucess. The preliminary injunction was issued. But they achieved several gains. The court did order the parties to engage in good-faith bargaining and kept an oversight on progress of the negotiation. And when the contempt motion was denied, teachers had been given a reprieve from legal sanctions—but only if the parties could soon reach agreement.

Finally, the action of the judge was much more diverse than the formal legal model would suggest. Judge Davis did issue the preliminary injunction but only after taking two previous actions: first, to deny the temporary restraining order and to allow a full hearing on the merits of the case, and second, to order the parties to negotiate in hopes that the pressure of possible court action and the scrutiny of progress in negotiation by the court might create added incentive to resolve the underlying dispute. Also, Judge Davis did not find teachers in contempt, believing that the parties were near resolution of the issues and that the issuing of contempt charges and sanctions would have heightened tensions rather than helped negotiations at that point.

In short, it was a combination of legal and extralegal factors and pressures—together with the relentless passage of time and the accumulation of inconvenience—that produced the serious bargaining that finally ended the dispute.

Review of Research on the Use of Injunctions

In this chapter, we have noted the transformation of the dispute that takes place when it is transferred from education to law, we have examined the injunctive process and the statutory and case law that governs and informs it, and we have examined that injunctive process in a hypothetical case: the Center City School strike. We need to ask one additional question about the injunctive process: What empirical studies have been conducted about teacher strikes in court and what are the findings?

There are relatively few extant studies of legal action in teacher-strike cases. Those studies that are available often are broader in scope (several cover public-sector strikes in general) or are limited in time and geography (often covering a particular strike or strikes in a specific jurisdiction or state). There are a series of descriptive and analytical accounts of particular strikes.[21]

Redenius surveyed thirty-nine public-sector strikes occurring in Wisconsin between May 1968 and October 1971. Fifteen of these were teacher strikes; in three, injunctions were issued. Redenius examined the views of parties on judicial mediation in injunction cases. He found that the majority of unions favored such mediation over the issuance of an injunction but the majority of governmental units did not. The majority of union attorneys also favored judicial mediation, but union leaders as a group did not. Redenius suggests that union leaders find judicial intervention damaging to the union.[22]

Gray and Dyson conducted research on the 353 public-sector strikes reported in the January 1970 through December 1971 issues of the *Government Employee Relations Report* on which information about imposition of a penalty for striking was available. The authors caution that these strikes may not be representative since it is possible that only major strikes were reported. They found that in 87 of the 353 strikes (25 percent), some form of court order was issued. In 46 of the 87 strikes (53 percent), injunctions were defied. Contempt proceedings were initiated in 33 cases of such noncompliance. Fines and jail sentences were levied against individuals in 20 strikes and fines against organizations in 9 strikes. Gray and Dyson note that partial or complete amnesty for strikers became a condition of settlement in many strikes and that some form of amnesty (either administrative or legal) was granted in 31 of the strikes. The authors conclude that the injunctive process and contempt proceedings do not necessarily deter public-sector strikes.[23]

Kaschock studied judicial processing of teacher strikes during the first thirteen months of operation of Pennsylvania's limited right-to-strike law, October 1970, through December 1971. He found fifty-six school strikes, in thirty-six of which injunctive relief was sought. He found that in eighteen of the thirty-six cases (50 percent) courts granted injunctions, in six cases (17 percent) the injunction was denied, and in twelve cases (33 percent) there was no judicial decision on the request for relief.[24]

Kaschock notes that a number of judges took an active role in the settlement of the dispute, requiring parties to return to the bargaining table and monitoring negotiations. He also found that judges used the threat of the issuance of an injunction to encourage settlement. Further, in two cases, judges took an even more direct role; in one, a judge imposed a salary settlement, and in another the judge ordered compulsory arbitration.

Colton studied 101 school strikes that occurred throughout the nation early in the 1975–1976 school year. Questionnaires were returned by the office of the superintendent in 89 percent of those districts. Colton found that 43 percent of these districts sought injunctive relief. The districts that went to court explained their actions as follows: They thought they had a legal obligation to do so (61 percent); they thought an injunction would put an end to the strike (50 percent); they thought going to court would bring the sides together (32 percent); and they believed an injunction would strengthen the board's position (16 percent). Districts that decided not to turn to the courts gave the following reasons: They simply did not seriously consider seeking court action (37 percent); they feared the judge would not issue an injunction (30 percent); they felt going to court would make a bad situation worse (27 percent); and they felt that the long-term costs of injunctions outweigh the potential short-term benefits (27 percent). Whether the district had sought an injunction or not, most were well satisfied with their course of action and would repeat that action, given another strike.

Colton found that in twenty-six of the districts, show cause hearings were held on contempt. He also found that large districts were more likely than small ones to be convinced that injunctions stop strikes, to seek injunctions, and to be the scene of contempt hearings.[25]

Finally, Graber conducted a study of all the elementary-school and secondary-school strikes in the nation during a twelve-month period (July 1, 1978, to June 30, 1979).[26] Questionnaires were sent to the superintendent of the 158 districts experiencing strikes: 129 were returned for a response rate of over 81 percent.

Ninety-one districts responding gave consideration to going to court; fifty-eight formally authorized such action and fifty-one filed a complaint or petition requesting an injunction. Of these, eight had an *ex parte* hearing only, twenty-six had a show cause hearing only, and fourteen had both an *ex parte* and a show cause hearing. There were thus requests for a total of twenty-two *ex parte* and forty show cause hearings. In two *ex parte* hearings, the request for court assistance was withdrawn before the judge issued a decision; this also occurred in three show cause hearings. This meant that judges issued decisions in twenty *ex parte* and in thirty-seven show cause hearings.

In twenty-eight instances, judges issued orders restricting picketing;

in fourteen instances (50 percent), teachers complied. In thirty-one instances, judges ordered teachers to return to the classroom; however, here teachers complied in only eleven instances (36 percent). In twenty districts (65 percent), teachers defied the orders of the court. It is such widespread noncompliance that led *The Washington Star* to editorialize that there is an increasing presumption that public-sector union employees will defy the courts.[27]

The results of the Graber research are discussed at greater length in subsequent chapters of the book in which the views and actions of the three parties to the court process—boards, teachers, and judges—are examined.

The studies reviewed here indicate that there are real decision dilemmas for the parties in the use of the injunctive process. Some districts seek injunctions and some do not. That choice must be weighed by boards as they try to anticipate, with the help of their legal counsel, what the consequences of seeking an injunction might be in the fluid complexity of an evolving teacher strike. For teachers too there are choices about how to defend themselves against charges and how to protect their claims and interests. And finally, there are decision dilemmas for the judge. The use of negotiation in place of or in addition to a formal legal decision indicates that the judge selects carefully among his options (or creates new options under the discretion accorded him in equity). The knowledge that many strikers in the public sector defy court orders also reaches backward to complicate the moment of decision for the judge.

It is to the exploration of such dilemmas facing the parties to the court action that we now turn.

Notes

1. There is a legal distinction between a court order to cease striking and one that orders teachers to return to the classroom. The former is prohibitory, the latter, mandatory. Mandatory injunctions are granted only in unusual circumstances. Judges often hesitate to issue a mandatory back-to-work order because of possible conflict with the Thirteenth Amendment proscription on involuntary servitude. However, since for the layperson the result is the same—if teachers cease striking, they return to work—we refer to the injunction as a "back-to-work order."

2. Comment, "Injunctions," *Harvard Law Review* 78 (1965):994–1093. See also John F. Dobbyn, *Injunctions* (Saint Paul, Minn.: West Publishing, 1974); and Donald H. Wollett and Robert H. Chanin, *The Law and Practice of Teacher Negotiations* (Washington, D.C.: Bureau of National Affairs, 1974).

3. Alan F. Westin and Barry Mahoney, *The Trial of Martin Luther King* (New York: Thomas Y. Crowell, 1974); Archibald Cox, "The New Dimensions of Constitutional Adjudication," *Washington University Law Quarterly* 51 (1976):791–829; and Owen M. Fiss, *The Civil Rights Injunction* (Bloomington, Ind.: Indiana University Press, 1978).

4. Fiss, *Civil Rights Injunction*, pp. 1–2.

5. Felix Frankfurter and Nathan Greene, *The Labor Injunction* (New York: Macmillan, 1930).

6. *United States v. United Mine Workers*, 330 U.S. 258.

7. *Norwalk Teachers' Association v. Board of Education*, 83 A.2d. 482, Conn. Sup. Ct. of Errors (1951):484–485.

8. Id. at 484.

9. *Manchester v. Manchester Teachers Guild*, 131 A.2d. 59, N.H. Sup. Ct. (1957):61–62.

10. *Pawtucket School Committee v. Pawtucket Teachers Alliance*, 141 A.2d. 624, R.I. Sup. Ct. (1958):626.

11. Id. at 628.

12. *School District for the City of Holland v. Holland Education Association*, 157 N.W.2d. 206, Mich. Sup. Ct. (1968).

13. Id. at 210.

14. Susan Frelich Appleton, "Appellate Review of Proceedings to Enjoin Teachers' Strikes: The Irreparable Harm Standard and Some Thoughts of the Perceived Benefits of Education," mimeographed (Saint Louis: Center for the Study of Law in Education, Washington Univeristy, 1980).

15. *School Committee of Westerly v. Westerly Teachers Association*, 229 A.2d. 441, Sup. Ct. of R.I. (1973):445.

16. Id. at 445.

17. *Timberlane Regional School District v. Timberlane Regional Education Association*, 317 A.2d. 555, Sup. Ct. of N.H. (1974):558.

18. Id. at 559.

19. *Joint School District No. 1 v. Wisconsin Rapids Education Association*, 234 N.W.2d. 289, Wis. Sup. Ct. (1975); and *School District No. 351 Oneida City v. Oneida Education Association*, 567 P.2d. 830, Sup. Ct. of Idaho (1977).

20. James H. Lytle and Jay M. Yanoff, "The Effects (if any) of a Teacher Strike on Student Achievement," *Phi Delta Kappan* 55 (December 1973):268.

21. Christopher R. Vagts and Robert B. Stone, *Anatomy of a Teacher Strike* (West Nyack, N.Y.: Parker, 1969); Donald J. Noone, *Teachers v. School Board* (New Brunswick, N.J.: Institute of Management and Labor Relations, Rutgers University, 1970); J.F. Halverson, *The Analysis of a Strike* (Bethesda, Md.: ERIC Document Reproduction Service, ED

046 068, 1970); Robert G. Stabile, *Anatomy of Two Teacher Strikes* (Cleveland: EduPress Publishing, 1974); David L. Colton, "The Influence of an Anti-Strike Injunction," *Education Administration Quarterly* 13 (Winter 1977):47–70; and Randal A. Lemke, "An Analysis of the Saint Louis Teachers' Strike: January to March, 1979" (Ph.D. dissertation, Washington University, Saint Louis, 1980).

22. Charles Redenius, "Participant Attitudes Toward Judicial Role in Public Employee Collective Bargaining," *Labor Law Journal* 25 (February 1974):94–113.

23. David A. Gray and B. Patricia Dyson, "Impact of Strike Remedies in Public Sector Collective Bargaining," *Journal of Collective Negotiations in the Public Sector* 5 (1976):125–132.

24. Alex Anthony Kaschock, "The Role of the Local Courts Under Pennsylvania's Public Employee Relations Act: October 1970 to January 1972" (M.A. thesis, Cornell University, 1977).

25. David L. Colton, "Why, When and How School Boards Use Injunctions to Stifle Teacher Strikes," *American School Board Journal* 164 (March 1977):32–35.

26. Edith E. Graber, "Survey of 1978–1979 Teacher Strikes," mimeographed (Saint Louis: Center for the Study of Law in Education, Washington University, 1980).

27. *Washington Star,* March 7, 1979.

4

School Boards as Petitioners

Initially a teacher strike is a political and organizational event, not a legal event. A strike is waged in the offices of the school system and the teachers' association, on the picket line, in the media, and in the reaction of community organizations, public officials, and individual citizens. The focal points are school operations and picketing, delineation of new bargaining positions, mobilization of third-party support, and neutralization of third-party opposition.

When teachers take a strike vote and begin a work stoppage, they have, by that action, seized the initiative in the collective-negotiation process and changed the nature of the dialogue. At that point, the initiative returns to the board.[1] What will be its reaction to the strike? A large number of choices and alternative courses of action present themselves. Many are nonlegal in nature. Shall the schools be kept open? Are there enough nonstriking teachers to do so? Can their number be supplemented by administrators, substitute teachers, and other personnel? How will communications with students and their families, with other school personnel, with the news media, and with the wider community be carried on? Can support personnel be persuaded to continue to provide their services? Should negotiations be resumed?

One of the courses of action open to the board is to seek an injunction that will order teachers back into the classroom. When the board prepares to take this action, it perceives the need for legal intelligence. This chapter begins with a discussion of the board's efforts to familiarize itself with the legal terrain. We next discuss pressures, both legal and nonlegal, both in the relationships with teachers and with the wider community, which favor and disfavor going to court. If the board decides to go to court, it will devise and execute tactics that assure that it will prevail in court. The board will also seek to settle the initial dispute through the added inducement of court pressures on teachers or will seek to quarantine the dispute by forcing the teachers back to work while negotiation continues. We consider how the board seeks to advance its case in the courtroom. Finally, we explore what happens when the court-ordered remedy is transferred back to the district for implementation.

A board does not calmly and rationally weigh and calculate all the factors discussed in this chapter. Events are crowding board members, school administrators, and legal counsel, and a dozen different matters need to be decided at once. Particular segments of the constituency are urging different courses of action. And the media representatives are at the door or on the telephone, wanting information for the next edition or newscast.

The pressures, experiences, and advice cited here are a composite gleaned from our interview with people who have experienced strikes and from observers. They reflect what they have learned about their experience or analysis of strikes and what they would take into account in a future similar situation.

Considering the Transfer to Law

School-board decisions about court action fall along a continuum. At one end are those boards whose immediate response to a strike is to transfer the dispute to the institution of law and to seek a quick court order. Indeed, in some strikes, boards apply for injunctive relief even before the strike has begun. For these boards, the decision to seek injunctive relief is relatively unproblematic. At the other end of the continuum there are districts for whom going to court is *not* a viable option. Nearly one-third of the districts in our 1978–1979 strike survey said they "did not consider" going to court. For a middle group the decision is contingent on varying situational factors. For these boards the questions are *whether* to go to court and *when*.

Legal Intelligence

If and when a board considers the option of injunctive relief, one of the first things that is apparent is that it needs information—legal intelligence. Since the institution of law is an unfamiliar one, the nonlegal observer may have unrealistic expectations of what a court can do and of what it is likely to do.

Faced with an unfamiliar institution, the board normally turns to experts. Many larger districts have legal counsel on their staff or have an ongoing contractual relationship with an attorney or a legal firm. In smaller districts, there may be an attorney (sometimes a county counsel or municipal attorney) who previously has been consulted or employed by the district. That attorney, if knowledgeable, can help narrow and refine the expectations of what can be accomplished by a quick resort to law.

There are strategic questions about which the board may want information. A Missouri board attorney explains:

A very strong factor, naturally is what effect will court action have on solving this labor dispute? Will it make matters worse? . . . Will strong action in court increase our chances of winning? Or will it make the teachers all that more determined to win, to hold out? There's that, always. . . . The feelings of the superintendent naturally have a lot to do with the course of conduct, but he doesn't necessarily call the shots. . . . He has a recommendation, but they [the board] all have their own feelings about that. And so they may or may not follow his recommendation. . . . They want to know what the lawyer thinks the litigation will do. Will it help? What problems will there be? What kind of judge will we get? Who are the possibilities? What are their backgrounds? How do they feel about unions?

An attorney also can answer the procedural questions that are outside the knowledge of the nonlegal person: what the first step is in "taking a case to court," how legal documents are prepared and what documents are needed, what kinds of facts and evidence should be cited, with which court the complaint should be filed.

The board is likely to weigh carefully what it learns from its attorney about the probable outcomes of going to court and of the requirements involved in taking this legal step. However, the attorney may have insufficient experience or may simply give wrong or unwanted advice. A school administrator's *Strike Manual* relates a "classic example": A board was advised by its attorney to fire all striking teachers. Two weeks later

after the board had created martyrs out of the strikers they realized that the Board would have to bring a dismissal action against every striker and that if they lost, it would cost millions of dollars. At that point, the Board settled the strike and rehired the strikers.[2]

In addition, the attorney may be well versed in school law but have little or no experience in labor law. An attorney with a Pennsylvania state school-board association remarks:

Most often in this state you still will find the local solicitor representing the school district in bargaining or with the board bargaining itself with the legal advice of a local solicitor. I by no means am trying to put down the competence of the local solicitor, but unless they have a practice devoted to labor law, I don't think they're cognizant of all the problems that they may face the first time around. And they go into court believing that it is in their best interest to go into court and believing that all they're going to get is an order that the teachers come back to work. When in reality they don't realize that the court may do a lot of things that they're not contemplating the court is going to do.

Some boards become independent consumers of legal services, seeking legal intelligence and counsel on their own to test whether there is agreement on the legal prognosis of their case. Or they may seek an attorney whose advice they like. In a New England strike-site study, the superintendent consulted three municipal attorneys in the face of an impending strike. All three doubted that the judge would ever grant an injunction. However, the superintendent consulted a fourth attorney who took the case and secured the injunction. In this case, the superintendent "shopped around" until he found an attorney who would pursue a chosen course of action. In another strike-site study, a school board discharged a legal firm and secured the services of another midway through a lengthy strike in order to pursue a strategy more to the board's liking.

Board attorneys also recognize that they need additional legal information. Many board attorneys begin their preparation for a strike long in advance of the event. In one site the attorney contacted the superintendent eight weeks before the strike, pointing out that there were a variety of legal problems that must be addressed and requesting that he be kept informed about staff planning. Two weeks later the attorney received a copy of the board's strike plan, detailing strategies for strike management and requesting advice on a series of law-related matters: treatment of pickets, termination of group-insurance policies, impact of a strike on state funding, legal ramifications of disciplinary action against striking teachers, and availability of injunctive relief. These queries prompted a good deal of research by the attorney and his colleagues. The attorney researched statutory and case law of that state and other states with regard to the legality of teacher strikes and prepared a series of memoranda. Most of these memos were summaries without legal interpretation. They were filed by the attorney to be accessible if and when needed. Two weeks before the strike began, the attorney wrote to the superintendent indicating that the legal research was largely completed and that henceforth legal information concerning the strike would be communicated orally (to prevent teachers from gaining access under provisions of the state's "sunshine law" governing public meetings and public documents).

Thus board attorneys recognize that they also need legal intelligence. In addition to their own research, they learn from the experiences of others. A Washington board attorney explains:

> You know, we attorneys work very closely together. . . . When there were strikes in September we were in almost daily contact with each other.

This attorney indicated that legal documents are also shared. He noted that he had immediately secured a copy of the judge's order issued in a neighboring strike and of teachers' pleadings in another district. He stated that "almost all of our briefs are pretty much the same," suggesting a standardization of the pleading and/or a borrowing from documents in other districts. Other information networks used by attorneys are the literature issued by state school boards' associations and conferences organized by school-board solicitors' associations. Thus both board members and legal counsel seek legal intelligence.

Pressures toward Court Action

A wide range of pressures and factors, both legal and nonlegal, enter into the board's decision as it weighs the option of seeking injunctive relief. We examine the nonlegal factors first. Not all of them are conducive to dispassionate rationality. A Missouri board member relates:

> It became very difficult in that we received threatening phone calls, other types of harassment. They marched up and down in front of our houses, carrying placards; they made threats against our families as well as our own person. It was a very difficult thing. We had women on the board who had never experienced a strike before in this school system . . . [and] it shook them up very badly and put them in an emotional strain. It was really bad.

There may be among board members some combination of partisanship and the will to win in adversary proceedings. One board attorney pointed out that once a strike or other controversy begins, there are some people who relish good combat. He noted, for instance, that a member of his board was a former athlete who simply loved to be in a competitive situation. The attorney indicated that a teacher strike lends itself to such an orientation and also to the orientation that sees issues in terms of good and evil. Such attitudes, he suggested, facilitate polarization and the exacerbation of the dispute.

The board may also view a lawsuit as a way of imposing punitive sanctions against teachers. There is an onus in being taken to court, in being charged with unlawful behavior, and in being judged as breaking the law. This onus may have decreased in an era of increasing litigation but, as we shall see, teachers reflect grave uneasiness in this situation. Whether additional sanctions of fines and/or jailing later follow, the reality of being taken to court may itself be perceived as a sanction. In this sense, it may be true as Feeley suggests, that "the process is the punishment."[3] Courts sometimes recognize the propensity of boards to be punitive. In a Michigan case, a judge wrote, "It is regrettable that the teachers have been lawless and the board vindictive."[4]

Beyond these expressive pressures that may incline a board toward court action are a variety of more rational considerations. The board has distinct organizational goals. One is to resume schooling as soon as possible. A Pennsylvania board attorney explains:

> Our clients in this really are the administration of the school district and the board of school directors. Their goal in a community like this is to get the kids back to school. So in representing our clients, the basic, number 1 aim or ambition that we have is to get the injunction in and get the kids back in school. Then we go back to the bargaining table with the teachers.

A Washington board attorney agreed that "what's really important is getting the teachers back and the students learning."

Even if this primary goal is not attained, an injunction still may serve broad objectives. Most important, an injunction may improve the board's bargaining position. An injunction will affirm the board's contention that teachers are engaged in illegal behavior and that law requires that they return to the classroom. Thus the injunction legitimates the board's position and brands teachers with the mark of illegality. Furthermore, an injunction expresses to the community the board's intention and determination to end the strike and creates the impression that it is the teachers who are frustrating resolution of the matter.

Another reason that boards go to court may be both to minimize the effectiveness of the current strike and also to deter future strikes. Their perception may be that if teachers feel they gained little in the current strike or that the gains were not worth the social and financial costs, they will be less likely to strike again. A New York Public Employee Relations Board attorney comments:

> There are many people who've written on the strike question and concluded that penalties are no deterrent at all. I think that's wrong. I think that New York's experience suggests that the plethora of penalties in New York, for better or for worse, has been a deterrent. . . . We have far less strikes than the experience in other states indicates that we should have. . . . It seems to me that the only explanation for that is the penalties.

To the extent that the board perceives penalties are providing a deterrent, they may go to court to facilitate that goal.

In addition, the board may perceive that nonstriking teachers (and even striking teachers) would welcome an injunction. A Pennsylvania superintendent explains:

Our teachers are essentially a law-abiding group in this matter and many, many of them wanted to return, but certainly they didn't want to return without having the backup of saying, "Well, I didn't really want to come back but I was forced to." And there are a few diehards of course who feel the other way. But essentially the staff was anxious to return. And they came back willingly.

The decision to go to court is influenced not only by the board's relationship with teachers but also by the community in which the strike is situated. Strong pressure for court action often comes from parents. A Pennsylvania State School Board Association attorney explains that the board may be

going to court as a result of being called on the phone every night by 30, 50 irate citizens to say, "Why the hell don't we get into court and get this thing stopped? Making arrangements to have my kids do something all day is a pain and I want them back in school." And I'm not sure exactly what part that plays in a strike. I know in the small areas and some of the suburban school districts around Harrisburg, everyone knows who's on the school board and whenever any problems arise, these people get phone calls. And if there are strikes they do get calls. It's probably difficult for them to say, "We're not going into court because if we go to court on a contract that you're not going to like . . ." when the people probably at that point are willing to say, "I don't care what you pay them, I'll complain about the taxes next year."

There may also be pressure from the state board of education to seek court action. In some recent Pennsylvania strikes, for instance, districts received a circular from the commissioner for basic education before the school year began, asserting that it was the department's view that students had a right to receive 180 days of instruction. He added that those districts that lost instructional days due to strikes "will be encouraged to seek court injunctions against any strike which would make it impossible for the students of those districts to receive 180 days of instruction this coming school year."[5] A school administrator also indicated that the state secretary of education had reminded districts "of the distinct obligation to provide 180 days of instruction." In view of this, a Pennsylvania superintendent asserted, "anything that encroaches on the 180 days of instruction must be challenged and examined."

Finally, in several strike sites, board representatives reflected their belief that if they did not take the dispute to court, some person from the community might do so. A Pennsylvania board attorney asserted:

Well, we believe here that if a board would fail to get or fail to seek an injunction, that a taxpayer would have standing to bring an action against the board in mandamus to require the board to do *something*.

We have thus far discussed nonlegal factors and pressures that may motivate a board to go to court. There are, in addition, some legal factors that encourage such a move. The first of these is the board's perception that it has a legal obligation to seek injunctive relief. This may be based on statutory law that encourages or mandates seeking an injunction in the event of a strike. In some states, boards have little discretion in the matter. New York State's Taylor Law, for example, requires a public employer to seek injunctive relief if employees strike.[6]

Even where the law does not specifically mandate seeking injunctive relief, a sense of legal obligation to do so may flow from the board's perception of its responsibility as officials in a local governmental unit. A Missouri board attorney explains:

> You know, one of the main things that's always on their mind is, what are their obligations in this kind of a situation? We're in a state where striking is illegal. There is no question about that. . . . Board members know and realize that they take an oath of office to uphold the law and one thing on their mind is, "Do I have either a legal or moral responsibility to see that the employees of this school system comply with the law?"

The sense of legal obligation also may arise from the fact that the length of the strike is threatening the possibility of being able to schedule the legally required 180 days of schooling. A Pennsylvania board attorney cites the example of a neighboring district:

> Our legal opinion to the board of school directors was that they ought to seek an injunction, that they have a legal duty to do this. . . . The [neighboring] school directors had not sought an injunction. . . . It was impossible at that time for them to complete the 180 days of school and Judge S. in his opinion, it seemed to us, indicated to the school district that they had a duty to come in and seek an injunction or seek to get everybody back in school. And that they had been lax in not doing this and not performing their duties. So it seemed to us that if you wanted to come into court in equity and you wanted to do so with clean hands . . . that you ought to come in before the 180 days ran.

An allied concern here is the possible loss of state subsidy if the required number of instructional days are not provided. A management attorney stated that the school board "would be lynched" if it lost state subsidy.

Another legal reason for going to court is to determine whether the charge of illegal behavior can be maintained. If so, there is then the basis from which other legal consequences and penalties may flow. An attorney with the New York Public Employee Board was asked:

> Q: Does the injunction in fact lead to the cessation of illegal activity?

A: Well, if it doesn't . . . it at least establishes a premise for penalizing the parties for their illegal activity which is an essential part, it seems to me, of a strike prohibition.

There is a final legal consideration that enhances the desirability of seeking injunctive relief. Boards usually win in court. Injunctive relief is seldom denied. On the other hand, as more and more boards are learning from experience or from their advisors, the victory may be so long delayed as to be of limited use, or it may produce no discernible improvement in the board's position vis-à-vis the teachers. We turn now to a discussion of these and other factors that may persuade a school board to avoid or delay efforts to seek injunctive relief.

Pressures against Court Action

The pressures that inhibit resort to the courts are, like those that encourage it, both nonlegal and legal in origin. Among the principal nonlegal factors are estimates about the effects of an injunction on board–teacher relationships. Teachers and administrators have cooperated on many levels in the past in pursuit of their common joint task: the education of the young. They will again join forces in the future since neither party can fulfill its work without the other. Taking the teachers to court may very well heighten and perpetuate tension between the parties. An appellate court noted this effect:

> The adversary posture of the parties in the courtroom setting creates a great deal of ill-will long after the dispute has ultimately been resolved.[7]

The after-strike environment is fragile enough without court action. The board may not want to increase that fragility. Moreover, a court order that merely brings the teachers back into the classroom leaves contract issues wholly or largely untouched. If teachers are back in the classroom and students are learning, the community may feel the matter has been "taken care of." But tensions between the parties may actually have been heightened by the adversary process. In such situations, "legal decisions may prematurely signal the end of conflicts without actually resolving them."[8]

We noted earlier that the board may not be motivated as much by the desire to preserve and restore amicable relationships with teachers as by an orientation that seeks to retaliate against what is perceived to be hostile action toward the board. Here too the decision not to go to court may recommend itself. If the board can keep the schools open with nonstriking teachers, support personnel and substitutes, then the requisite

180 days continue to run, and striking teachers are missing a day's pay for each day they are absent from work. This produces economic pressure on the teachers to end the strike. A Pennsylvania board attorney notes:

> There's always some feeling on those boards, you know, to "Let them sit. Who cares? Let them lose money." . . . The real intent of these districts in letting the 180 days run is to punish the teachers, to be quite frank with you. . . . There are a lot of school-board members who feel, "If they are out on strike, let them stay out for a while and let them lose some money as I would if I were working in a mill or anywhere else."

In addition to weighing how court action may affect relationships with teachers, the board must also assess whether community opinion and pressures support court action. Here also it may be wise to delay court action as long as possible.

The nature of the community in a particular strike may make it advisable to proceed to court very cautiously or not at all. In a 1979 Saint Louis strike, a predominantly black teachers' union was striking against a predominantly white school board. Students and school patrons were also predominantly black. Before the strike, racial tensions had been heightened over the closing of a hospital in the black residential area of the city, mandated by a largely white city administration. Now there was a school strike with a set of white attorneys, a predominantly white board, and a white superintendent. In this instance, the school board first initiated and then withdrew a request for injunctive relief. The board did not return to court until forced to do so well into a lengthy strike by a parents' suit.

In addition to nonlegal considerations, there are legal ones that may militate against seeking an injunction. We have noted that the injunction will likely be issued; this is a factor that recommends court action. But the matter is not so simple. In initiating court action, the board triggers a series of legal steps that may be difficult to halt or reverse. If the injunction is issued, the teachers may or may not comply. If they do not, the court may expect the board to initiate contempt charges. Indeed, in the 1978 Everett (Washington) strike, the court declined to issue injunctive relief until the board presented its enforcement plan. Or the court may seize the initiative, instituting contempt proceedings on its own motion. If teachers are found in contempt of court and jailed, the board is left with limited options in reinstituting negotiations and may need to make some concessions in order to break the deadlock. A staff member of the New York Public Employee Relations Board described such a strike:

> The union leader there was jailed by the judge. . . . [W]e were able

to go into chambers and with the acquiescence of the school board get the fellow released from jail to resume negotiations. . . . There were no negotiations without this guy. That's all there was to it. Just nothing was moving, and nothing *could* move without him. He was martyred, he was in jail, the union did all the things unions do, and nothing was happening. Here we were into like forty days of strike. . . . [W]e thought the public interest would be served by assisting in getting his release. . . . I think we had twenty-four-hour release. We went back to negotiations . . . and the thing resolved itself.

Such a course of events does not enhance the bargaining position of the board. The union has held both board and court at bay and demonstrated that it must be listened to and its positions taken into account. In a 1970 Los Angeles strike, a trial-court judge fined but did not jail union leaders. Rather, he called on the legislature to legislate stiffer sanctions for those who refuse to comply with court orders. He asserted that he did not jail teachers because "it is exactly what they seek . . . a martyr's cloak." As a Washington attorney explains, boards may be reluctant to commit themselves to the full progression of legal events that is initiated with the filing of the complaint:

School districts don't like to have their hands tied. They like to get the injunction, force the teachers back to work. But they don't want to really go in and enforce the injunction through contempt or fines or jail.

On occasion the tables may be turned. A board ready to press contempt charges may encounter a judge who is reluctant to incarcerate or fine the teachers. Where either the board or the judge is not willing to "go the distance," one party may be frustrated and angry with events and may hold the other accountable for the outcome of the case. This is a matter to which the board may want to give some thought before filing a complaint with the court. A Vermont superintendent advises:

If you're willing to undertake the pressures that go with a strike, then get in it and get in it to win. If you're not willing to take those pressures, if you feel you'll buckle under them, then settle before the strike begins.

But even if the board is willing to press matters, the court may not be. An Illinois attorney relates:

We already had the experience in 1976 where the judge just wouldn't rule on anything. He used the excuse that there was some technicality in the complaint, which was minor to the extent that we could have orally amended it right then. . . . We knew in the present strike that the court might fail to grant us any form of relief by simply finding

some reason to delay. . . . . I dare say that problems I've heard about
. . . where school districts have been denied the injunction or where
they've been put off unmercifully, has to do not so much with the fact
that the attorney for the board is not prosecuting it diligently, but rather
the court just won't face up to it for one reason or another. And there
are just so many reasons the court can give for putting us off that you
could be denied an injunctive order almost forever.

Even in states where statutory law mandates securing an injunction, a
judge may delay the court order for a short period of time. Most often
the judge's intention in delaying the order is to allow other settlement
processes to operate. That may negate the purpose for seeking injunctive
relief in the first place.

Board members reflect that another factor suggesting caution in the
use of the legal process is that the judge may become involved in the
case in ways the board had not intended. Boards anticipate that the judge
will function as an impartial adjudicator of the legal dispute, that is, the
strike. But the judge may perceive that a court order will not resolve the
strike and may even heighten tensions. He or she may believe that court
orders will be defied. Many courts are reluctant to issue orders that are
difficult to enforce. The judge may have prolabor leanings or perceive
that the justice of the case lies with teachers even though the law favors
the board. Thus the judge may find it attractive to try to resolve the
bargaining dispute rather than the legal dispute about the strike itself.

Board sources reflect uneasiness about what they perceive to be a
widening of the role of the judge. A Pennsylvania board attorney reports:

> Our opinion . . . is that the courts ought not to get involved in the
> negotiations. As a matter of fact, we're afraid of that to some extent.
> We don't want the court getting in . . . making public the offers and
> . . . getting us into the public's view because . . . our opinion is that
> the school directors have an obligation to negotiate with these teachers,
> number 1. And that, number 2, they have the duty to watch the public
> purse strings. And once you get it out in the public and so on, there's
> often more pressure to, well, just pay them what they want and get it
> settled. . . . [Judge X] locks people in chambers . . . and orders them
> to negotiate for twenty-six hours or whatever you will, and then they
> come out half dead with some sort of settlement without much thought
> going into it on either side. And it seems to me if you're going to have
> free collective bargaining, you can't have it judicially imposed
> . . . . [Another judge in the Y school district] ordered them to meet
> three times a week at the school for so many hours. Well, through the
> rumor mill, it came back to us that, yes, they were meeting three times
> a week. One group would meet in one room and play cards. The other
> group would meet in another room and watch television. So that kind
> of collective bargaining is no good, and the courts have no business
> getting involved in it.

A New York state labor-relations board attorney observes it is difficult for the judge to combine the roles of adjudicator and mediator in the same case:

> Judges have what would appear to be some kind of conflict here in terms of mediating on the one hand and on the other hand, imposing penalties, without any statutory distinction between the two. . . . On the one hand, . . . they have the responsibility to impose penalties if [court orders] are violated. And at the same time they assume the role of mediator, conciliator, trying to put it together.

A judge may also become involved in the case in other ways. Although most judges will not become directly involved in contract issues, some judges do. A judge may decide to order or impose an interim contract while negotiations continue. Thus the judge may influence or structure not only the negotiation process but also the outcome of that process. In this sense the judge moves in the direction of imposing conditions on the parties. In one such instance Pennsylvania board sources felt that the judge had "gone beyond his discretion to order them back under the terms and conditions of the prior contract." A step increase is normally granted to teachers each year based on the acquisition of another year of experience. It was the board's position that this increase was one of the matters to be bargained. The judge's action had removed this item from the negotiations.

In another case a judge introduced an issue that had not been argued by the parties. Subsequently the case took "a life of its own," assuming a direction that the board had not anticipated. In the 1978 Butler Area School District strike (Pennsylvania), the board had brought a conventional injunctive petition, seeking to have the court order teachers back to the classroom. The judge did so but then, in a surprise move, declared the Public Employee Relations Act (PERA) of Pennsylvania unconstitutional:

> The strike provisions of PERA relating to public school teachers cannot be reconciled with the Public School Code and the Constitution of Pennsylvania. The portion of PERA legalizing strikes by public school teachers is unconstitutional.[9]

Thereafter, in the words of a board representative, the constitutional issue "mushroomed and became the whole case." And once the judge had raised the issue, the district "was obligated to follow through. No way we could avoid it. . . ." The case eventually was heard by the Pennsylvania Supreme Court where the justices, in a *per curiam* decision, held that the trial-court judge's ruling that PERA was unconstitutional,

was "improvident . . . and is declared of no effect."[10] In this case, the
board got much more legal action than it anticipated when it filed its
petition for an injunction.

The judge may also rule against the board or may criticize the board
in court or both. In a Washington case, the judge found that the board
had engaged in bad-faith bargaining; he agreed to use the injunction
only on the condition that the school board resign. In a California case,
teachers were listened to sympathetically in court, but board representatives were told that the judge did not want to hear from them. A board
attorney reported that the judge finally granted the injunction but told the
board, "If you try to enforce it, now that you've got me involved, I'm
going to settle the strike." He then attempted to find more money for the
board to give teachers.

Or the judge may decide to deny the board's request for a court order.
A school administrator suggests that the board is in an uncomfortable
position if the court refuses to issue the injunction it is requesting:

> By failing to obtain the sought-after order, the strike takes on an aura
> of legitimacy and the organization will publicize the fact that the strike
> is legal (even though it is not) and claim a major "victory" for its
> followers.[11]

The probability of such an outcome is low—particularly in the states
where statutes clearly outlaw teacher strikes or where the case law clearly
indicates that public-employee strikes warrant issuance of injunctions.
But there are many states where the law is not clear or where it is
altogether silent. In one state where neither the courts nor the legislature
had spoken, a board attorney counseled delaying court action as long as
possible, not because he thought that injunctive relief would be denied,
but because he believed that an adverse decision—even though highly
unlikely—should be avoided if at all possible. It would, he noted, affect
not only the present strike but also any subsequent ones.

In sum, the process of weighing the relative advantages and disadvantages of going to court is not an easy one. The reasons for seeking
injunctive relief may be outwardly persuasive, but the risks are real too.
Sometimes it is events, rather than a rational calculation, that determine
whether a board goes to court. Many strikes are of such short duration
that they are over before the board can complete a process of considering
and approving court action. In states where there is a limited right to
strike, settlements sometimes occur within the "window" period in which
the strike may not be enjoined. In other states the statutes may require
a board to seek injunctive relief, quite aside from the board's own pref-
erences. The threat of a parent suit may force a board's hand.

We do not know the precise proportion in which emotion, cold calculation, and necessity determine board decisions to seek or not to seek injunctive relief. We do know that in the 1978–1979 teacher strikes about 30 percent of school districts reported that they did not consider going to court, that another 30 percent considered the matter but for one reason or another did not take the step of filing a request for an injunction, and that the remaining 40 percent considered the idea, approved it, and then officially requested injunctive relief. It is to this latter group of districts that we now turn as we examine their efforts to mobilize the law.

The Board Goes to Court

With the transfer of the strike to court, the board transmits the case to legal actors. Much of the momentum in the handling of the case lies with the board's attorney. Nevertheless, board members have some roles to play in the guidance and support of the case.

In chapter 3 we presented a typical injunction hearing. Here we review and highlight several key factors in the show cause hearing that are of concern to the board.

Timing

A panel of school-board representatives who had been involved in teacher strikes agree that "timing was the most crucial factor to consider in seeking legal action."[12] The significance of timing stems from a number of considerations. Whether teachers defy an eventual court order may be influenced by when the board goes to court. A Washington board attorney explains:

> Rushing into court at the drop of a pin is . . . probably doomed to failure in many circumstances simply because psychologically the teachers are not ready to be ordered back. There's the euphoria that goes with hitting bricks . . . in effect, the emotional release of voting for a strike and seeing the strike vote win. And getting out there with your signs and so forth. If you attempt to stop that too quickly, you are simply being premature in your use of what can be a very effective tool.

Another consideration is public opinion. A Michigan school administrator reports:

> We didn't go for an injunction right away. School was supposed to start on Tuesday and we didn't go to court until Friday of the following

week. . . . We didn't want to go to court too soon, before we began
to get some pressure building up in the community. But by the second
week of the strike . . . pressure was building in the community. We
began to get some inquiries: Why don't you go to court?

Hence there may be a value in delaying court action. On the other hand,
it is also possible to wait too long. We have noted that one board attorney
felt a neighboring district had waited too long in seeking an injunction
and that the judge had criticized the board, indicating that they ought to
apply for relief when the length of the instructional year was threatened.
A strike-management consultant suggested it might be well for the board
to hold out and try all other remedies first and then say to the judge,
"Look, we tried everything else. We waited it out. We negotiated with
teachers. We can't get them back. Now we're coming to you for an
injunction." This may impress the judge. On the other hand, as one
observer noted, the judge may also ask "If it's so urgent, why did you
wait so long?"

School boards' sense of timing can be upset by attempts at intervention
by third parties. For example, in a Washington teacher strike, a petition
for injunctive relief filed by a group of students had the effect of accel-
erating the school board's own schedule for requesting such relief. In the
1979 Saint Louis teacher strike a group of parents, impatient with the
board's failure to seek court relief, successfully filed a motion of their
own, virtually forcing the board to do likewise.

Interaction with the Judge

We noted earlier that the board, in its assessment of whether to go to
court, seeks to know as much as possible about the attitude of the judge
before whom the case is to be heard. As the case proceeds, the board
gains additional information; the board may wish to modify its strategy
on the basis of this additional data. A board attorney in a midwestern
state comments:

Let me say that I suppose the important matter in seeking injunctive
relief is what judge is going to have it. And since attorneys have little
participation in the selection of the judge, that is difficult to advise. It
makes the matter difficult. . . . But I would say that you should have
some concept of what . . . the judge's attitude is before you decide
how far and to what extent to press the matter. . . . We really have
had two experiences in school strikes. [In the other one] the judge who
was involved was a judge who had come up from representing a number
of unions. And it was obvious that what he intended to do was to stall
until the thing was settled. And with that we saw the handwriting on

the wall. . . . So I would say that one of the most important things is to know, as much as possible, the attitude of the judge.

The Argument in Court

As noted earlier, where statutes or case law clearly indicate that teacher strikes are illegal, the board has a strong base for its claim. In states where strikes are allowed, they may still be found to be illegal if not all the prerequisites have been met. The situation is somewhat more difficult where case law and statutes are silent on the legality of strikes. In those cases, boards' attorneys prepare lengthy legal memoranda designed to persuade the court to use *Norwalk* and similar cases as precedent to find that the strike is illegal and should be enjoined.

A concurrent argument in many cases is that of irreparable harm. We noted in chapter 3 that a traditional prerequisite for injunctive relief is the showing that the action cited in the complaint will result in irreparable (noncompensable) harm. Some courts have held that an illegal strike is per se harmful and that harm need not be shown. Nevertheless, some attorneys make the argument:

Q: On the one hand you appear to argue that you don't have to show harm and then you proceed to say "There is a lot of harm and the affidavits support that."

A: That's called arguing in the alternative. And that simply means that when you go to court, you do not want to give away anything. So you go into court and you say, "Your Honor, the law does not require us to show irreparable harm. That's our position. But if Your Honor rules that the law does require us to show irreparable harm, here is the irreparable harm." It simply means that we're prepared to argue any position that the court feels we have to argue.

Some jurisdictions require at least a cursory showing of harm, and others may require a strong showing.[13] The arguing of harm is not a simple matter. A board attorney notes:

The evidentiary part of these hearings often is difficult. A lot of what you're asking the administrator to testify about—and that's basically who you have, the administrators—is nothing more than their opinion. . . . You have administrators testifying about what effect this will have on the average child or what effect this will have on those who want to go to college, and it's kind of a speculative situation because they're speculating on whether or not colleges will admit those students without them having fully completed the school year.

This same attorney indicated that hard evidence was difficult to procure:

> Data would be extremely helpful. In most cases it's not available. Except
> that it is available in reference to retarded or emotionally disturbed
> children in the form of experts' opinions that a break in the continuity
> of a program . . . has a tremendously adverse effect on this child or
> on the class as a whole. . . . And this is about the only area where
> we had any evidence if you will. . . . As to regular, normal, everyday
> school children, what effect it has on them is basically speculation.

One solution to the problem of insufficient evidence is adroitness on
the witness stand. A superintendent reports his experience:

> I don't know how many hours their attorney cross-examined me. . . .
> I project one hour for every minute of knowledge that I have. . . . He
> wanted to know if I had anything to substantiate [an assertion that the
> strike adversely affected the perceptions of primary-school children].
> I said to him, ''Yes, I can locate it if I can be released from here''. . . .
> I knew I could get him by now; I'd learned this. . . . This released
> me; he backed off. He really thought I could come up with it. I did
> have some information. . . , but it was not a study that had been
> conducted.

Another tactic is to simply pile up the list of alleged harms. A board
attorney reports:

> If you can collect a number of things and throw all these effects into
> one big ball, that cumulative effect may in itself present a clear and
> present danger. So we throw in all these various things such as . . .
> the cafeteria workers won't get paid, the bus drivers won't get
> paid. . . . Working mothers have to stay home. . . .

But such compilations produce risks of their own, for teacher attorneys
can consume precious hours of courtroom time in cross-examining board
witnesses and in introducing witnesses who will counter those presented
by the petitioners.

Setting the Solution Back

Taking a teacher-strike case to court involves disengaging the dispute
from its original setting, transferring it to law through the injunctive
process, having it adjudicated there, and then sending the solution back
in the institution of origin.[14] The question then arises, will the teachers
comply? If not, then what?

Neither boards nor courts are always willing to use the full panoply of law and the full extent of the legal process to prosecute teachers. Sanctions quickly become counterproductive when the strike relationship has already heightened tensions and widened existing divisions. A Missouri board attorney explains:

> After the strike is settled, the school board wants peace. And by pursuing those penalties you only aggravate the personnel problem. And so the tendency is to let it lie.

Similarly, a New York board attorney finds:

> As part of the settlement of the strike, there is the desire to get it over with. And many chief legal officers simply don't go back to court to get contempt. They will take $10,000, $5,000, a fine against the union, no fines against individuals, that sort of thing. There have been some rather severe penalties in fines. But they are usually in the lengthier strikes. Judges, like chief legal officers, and politicians, they're influenced by arguments of "Let's get it behind us" and quite often the penalties are not assessed or they're modified.

A Washington teacher attorney indicates that if the judge wants to be punitive, it may be necessary for attorneys to attempt to divert such action:

> You've got to hold a judge back if you see he's coming down too much for you and the school district's got to do the same thing. If a judge gets too angry at teachers, the board's got to hold him back because they know that the action is going to be the reverse of what's expected. Sure, they'll get an order to return to work, but they're going to have teachers so solid against them that they'll never do it. They'll never settle. So you sometimes have to tone things down. In X's case it worked the other way. The judge was a little too tough on the board.

As part of the negotiation process after noncompliance, the teachers usually demand, and the board often agrees to amnesty from board sanctions. The noncompliance thus becomes an additional matter of negotiation to be addressed by the board and the court.

Board Evaluation of Court Action

In view of the many complexities and uncertainties of court action, it is hardly surprising to find petitioners who express reservations about the utility of injunctions. Some recognize that a strike is but a symptom and indication of an underlying dispute that is not formally before the court.

As a Missouri board attorney noted, ''This is a situation that's not going to be settled in court. It's not a legal problem, basically.'' And an Illinois attorney concludes,

> I have the view that the entire injunctive relief process is inadequate. There has to be some statutory change made where we either have a collective-bargaining law which requires some mediation or arbitration or something. . . . Injunctive relief is so slow, so tedious, and so much left to the discretion of the judge that the school board is effectively without a really good remedy.

A Washington board attorney describes the strike in which he was involved using the analogy of a war on three fronts: the collective-bargaining process, court action, and the strategy of reopening the schools during the strike. Of the three fronts, he felt that the court action was the least effective.

Not all attorneys agree, however. In the 1978–1979 strike survey, superintendents were asked to evaluate the contribution of the court to the resolution of their dispute. Of the forty-seven districts that responded, 23 percent found the court indispensable to the resolution of the dispute, another 23 percent found the court was of substantial assistance but not indispensable, 36 percent found the court of some assistance, 11 percent said the court was of no assistance, and 6 percent indicated that the court had complicated negotiations and made revolution difficult. Thus while nearly one-fourth of the districts found court assistance indispensable, another 60 percent indicated the court had provided at least some assistance.[15]

When queried whether they would recommend court action in a next strike, 82 percent of districts that went to court indicated that they would ''definitely'' or ''probably'' do so and 18 percent said they would not. Of the districts that did not take their dispute to law, 58 percent said they would urge a similar course in another strike.

When the two measures (evaluation of court action and recommendation of action in another strike) were combined, it was found that two factors explained a positive response in both areas: The positive group was more than twice as likely to have received an injunction that was honored by teachers, and they were more than twice as likely to have had some type of judicial involvement in settlement attempts.

Some attorneys comment on their positive experience with the court. A Washington board attorney notes:

> I'm very pleased [with the action the court took]. I am convinced the strike would not have ended without the court action. [The strike] was a mistake. It was blundered into by the district and the teachers. There

was a little bit of gamesmanship towards the end of the summer, and it got to be who could draw faster and who would blink first. So consequently we blundered in the strike, and I think the district shares some of the blame for that. . . . Once the strike started, the district got its act together very quickly. The teachers did not. And as the strike wore on, the teachers' union fell apart. . . . I don't think there was another way of ending the strike without a strong, forceful court order.

And a midwestern superintendent said he would advise any district to go to court. One factor, he said, was that, in the eyes of the public, you have to pursue every available means of ending the strike, and securing a court order is an obvious way to do this. He was especially pleased with the way the court had brought the parties back to the bargaining table. Both the superintendent and the board attorney in the case, in separate interviews, indicated that they had asked the judge to issue a statement, urging the parties to negotiate. The superintendent asserted that this constituted normal action for the judge who is accustomed to working in chambers to "engineer settlements of disputes." Negotiations continued in chambers until settlement two days later. The attorney added:

I think we both were of the opinion that in this state the real test of the efficacy of an injunction proceeding is whether or not it promotes a settlement rather than whether or not an injunction is issued.

Board representatives with whom we spoke thus revealed that there are certain risks and unanticipated consequences that need careful scrutiny before going to law and careful maneuvering while in court.

Notes

1. The term *board* is used here in a collective sense. It incorporates not only the members of the school board who carry legal responsibility for the suit but also those persons designated by the board to carry out its task, namely, school administration officials and legal counsel.

2. Association of California School Administrators, *Strike Manual* (Burlingame, Calif.: Association of California School Administrators, 1973), pp. 64–65.

3. Malcolm M. Feeley, *The Process is the Punishment* (New York: Russell Sage, 1979).

4. Brief in Support of Complaint for Mandamus, *Irwin v. Ecorse Board of Education*, No. 118598, Cir. Ct., Wayne County, Mich. (September 26, 1968).

5. Frank S. Manchester, Commissioner for Basic Education, *Basic*

Education Circular 34-78, Commw. of Pa., Dept. of Education (August 15, 1978).

6. Chapter 392 of the Laws of 1967, as amended, Section 211 provides that when public-sector workers are on strike, "the chief legal officer of the government involved shall forthwith apply to the supreme court for an injunction against such violation."

7. *Joint School District No. 1 v. Wisconsin Rapids Education Association,* 234 N.W.2d. 289, Wis. Sup. Ct. (1975):300.

8. Austin Turk, "Law as a Weapon in Social Conflict," *Social Problems* 23 (February 1976):286.

9. Reproduced Record, *Butler Area School District v. Butler Education Association,* 6 Butler L.J., (C.P. Butler, 1978):113–114.

10. *Butler Area School District v. Butler Education Association,* 391 A.2d. 1295, Pa. Sup. Ct., (1978).

11. Association of California School Administrators, *Strike Manual,* p. 8.

12. Jo Love Beach, "Strikes Reviewed," *Compass,* November–December 1978 (Olympia, Wash.: Washington State School Directors' Association):24.

13. Susan Frelich Appleton, "Appellate Review of Proceedings to Enjoin Teachers' Strikes: The Irreparable Harm Standard and Some Thoughts of the Perceived Benefits of Education," mimeographed (Saint Louis: Center for the Study of Law in Education, Washington University, 1980).

14. Paul Bohannan, "Law and Legal Institutions," *International Encyclopedia of the Social Sciences* 9 (1968):73–78.

15. Edith E. Graber, "Survey of 1978–1979 Teacher Strikes," mimeographed (Saint Louis: Center for the Study of Law in Education, Washington University, 1980).

5 Teachers as Respondents

Teachers have developed strategies designed to impede school-board efforts to use injunctive relief. These strategies are not based on the expectation of winning the legal battle. Such a goal would be unrealistic in view of the fact that injunction proceedings that are carried to final judicial resolution almost always are decided in favor of petitioners. Instead, the teachers seek to delay, deflect, or defy injunctions so that they do not damage their strike. In addition, teachers seek to turn injunction proceedings to their own advantage by involving the court in efforts to break the impasse with the board of education. These goals are pursued both inside and outside the courtroom.

Strategy

Teacher-organization attorneys readily acknowledge that they are unlikely to prevail in an injunction proceeding. Trial courts rarely dismiss injunction requests, and appellate courts rarely overturn injunctions that have been issued. Consequently, teacher-association attorneys have a rather prosaic conception of their role. A teacher attorney in Washington puts it this way:

> I'm a hired gun. I'm just part of the overall concept of what's going on. They hired me to do one thing, and that was to try and prevent the restraining order from coming into existence. Second, in the event the restraining order comes into existence, help us as much as you can to mitigate any kind of problem to us. You know, just because an order is issued, you don't drop the client. . . . You go in and you argue the reasons why the judge shouldn't throw him in the slammer. That's the second part of my job. And thirdly, we are hired to do what we can to put pressure on the school district to get in and negotiate in good faith. If we can delay, if we can stall, if we can make them look silly, then that puts pressure on. It's all a very dynamic situation.

The delay theme is a pervasive one among teacher-organization attorneys. For example, a Pennsylvania attorney describes his strategy in these terms:

> First of all he files every kind of legal paper he can . . . to give them

another day, another twenty-four hours, another two or three days—
anything that gives them time. Delay, delay, delay, to be truthful. I
hate to call it that, but that's what it means. . . . We try everything
there is to delay to give us time, time, time. Because you never know
what happens in time. Sometimes someone will get to the school
board. . . . Time always works for the union, works against the employer. Unless the employer can starve them out. They can't in many
instances.

However, delay is not an absolute virtue. Some strike organizers contend
that an injunction must be issued and then defied in order to convince
management that it really must reopen negotiations. A Missouri attorney
notes:

Our clients were interested in a confrontation with management, believing that this would lead to an early settlement. We were not to delay
the injunction process.

A Washington attorney also was skeptical about the virtues of delay,
contending that a school board seeking injunctive relief was not likely
to alter its bargaining position until the request for relief had been granted
or denied by the court. In Michigan a strike leader explained that initial
delay was desirable in order to give the teacher organization time to
prepare its members to respond to the injunction; however, the delay was
not to be so long that the injunction came after rank-and-file teachers had
become worn out or discouraged by their strike. Delay then seems to be
a strategy that is selectively useful, depending on the circumstances.

A second goal is to protect teachers from sanctions. Fines levied
against individuals or teacher organizations are to be avoided. However,
there is some ambivalence about jail sentences. While a jail term may
be personally unpleasant, the event can be used to create martyrs whose
predicament provides further fuel for the strike.

A third goal is to try to limit the scope of whatever injunction is
issued. One teacher attorney puts it this way:

Thinking about the role of the lawyer in a teacher case . . ., I think
realistically where we have the most effect is to try to minimize the
effect of the order, to minimize findings and conclusions to keep the
door as wide open for the next case as possible. . . . We worked very
hard to [limit the terms of the injunction].

Beneath these specific strategic goals, there lies a unifying orientation. It is that the legal dispute is to be contained or manipulated in
ways that maintain the primacy and the viability of the underlying
teacher–board dispute, and which redirect attention to that dispute. If the

teachers are to return to work, they want the return to be the result of a negotiated agreement, not an injunction. To achieve that overriding goal, teacher attorneys try to take advantage of any opportunities they find within the injunction process.

Courtroom Proceedings

Whereas most school boards have ready and regular access to attorneys, most teacher organizations do not. For teacher organizations, access to legal assistance usually is through a handful of designated attorneys scattered throughout a state. Each one is responsible for providing legal services to several teacher units. Arrangements vary considerably from state to state. In Washington, Michigan, and Pennsylvania, for example, the state-level unit of the National Education Association (NEA) maintains a network of attorneys who are in private practice throughout the state; when an injunction is filed against a teachers' association, an attorney from the network is assigned to handle the response. In New York State the principal teachers' organization is an AFT unit; it employs a group of more than twenty attorneys who service the state's several hundred affiliated teacher-bargaining units.

Because teachers' attorneys are not employed by individual bargaining units, they rarely are involved in the extended negotiations that usually precede a strike, and they are unfamiliar with the key local actors and issues in particular situations. If a strike occurs or an injunction is filed against the teachers, preparation of a legal response often is on very short notice. An attorney summoned to defend teachers in a big city strike wryly describes the extent of his prior preparation:

We were not notified about the strike or about anything to do with the bargaining until the morning that they took the strike vote. They called us, and—I can remember their words—they said, "Well, Bob, we've got a strike." I couldn't believe it. Because everything I'd heard was that there wasn't going to be a strike. I wasn't involved in the bargaining issues. I didn't know anything about them. I'd read it. I'd followed it in the newspapers. But I didn't really know what their issues were. I didn't know whether there had been bad-faith-bargaining instances because they handle all of these unfair labor practice things pretty much by themselves or through [their state organization]. So they call you up and they say, "Bob we've got a strike. We're hitting the bricks in half an hour." Which means two things. First of all, you're going to be called into the picture to bail them out if they have to go to court. And secondly, nobody's going to be available to work on the legal case. They're all out doing picket signs, organizing demonstrations, you know—all the many, many things that have to be done in a strike. And that's all they want to focus their attention on.

This attorney's situation is not at all unique. At a show cause hearing in an Illinois district, we observed the teachers' attorney—brought in on short notice from the state's capital where he resided—being introduced to named defendants in the courtroom just moments before the hearing began. Stabile reports a teacher-organization officer's account of a similar occurrence:

> The hearing was kind of a surprise to me. We went down to the meeting not knowing what to expect. I hadn't met the lawyer previous to that morning. I had coffee and toast with him then. We went into court and their lawyer called me to the stand at nine o'clock, and I was there until twelve o'clock. I really hadn't expected to be on the stand at all.[1]

The absence of advance warning and of time for preparation is of little immediate significance in situations where orders are granted on an *ex parte* basis. There, by definition, respondents' attorneys have no opportunity to address the court prior to issuance of its order. Instead, teacher attorneys concern themselves with the problem of defending against sanctions if the injunction is defied. In addition, they prepare for the preliminary hearing that usually follows an *ex parte* order within a matter of days.

In preliminary hearings, whether or not preceded by issuance of an *ex parte* order, teacher attorneys avail themselves of what one attorney called a "smorgasbord of defenses." They include challenges to the court's jurisdiction as well as arguments based on traditional restraints on judicial use of equitable powers. The restraints involve such matters as the legal status of strikes, the availability of alternative forms of relief, the validity of claims that a strike is irreparably harmful, the extent to which the petitioner has "clean hands," and the "balancing of the equities." Opportunities for further tactical maneuvers arise in connection with enforcement of injunctions. The following sections describe the manner in which these tactics are employed by teacher attorneys in their efforts to forestall injunctions and to turn injunction proceedings to the advantage of their clients.

Jurisdiction

The jurisdiction of courts is limited. It extends only to people and issues properly before the court. Normally, petitioners take precautions to ensure that proceedings will not be delayed or dismissed over jurisdictional issues, but occasionally teacher attorneys, outwardly paying homage to "proper procedure," find opportunities to raise questions. In an Illinois case a teachers' attorney, seeking delay and simultaneously seeking to limit the scope of any injunction that might issue, challenged the petitioners' designation of defendants. The board's petition named as defendants the local education association (as an entity) and several of its officers. Then in the main body of the petition the board declared that its petition was a class action that included as defendants all members of the association plus "all other persons who have acted in participation, combination, concern and sympathy with the named individual defendants." When he filed his response, and in subsequent oral argument, the teachers' attorney contended that under Illinois law the persons whom the board sought to enjoin were not numerous enough to constitute a class, that the named defendants were not properly representative of the class inasmuch as some teachers were not members of the teachers' association, some were not tenured, and "some may have various and sundry defenses such as illness." The petitioners, the attorney suggested, should have asked the court for a determination as to the appropriateness of a class action and as to the membership in the class. But the board had failed to do so, and so the teachers asked that the petition be dismissed or, in the alternative, modified. In any event, the attorney said he represented only the teachers whose names appeared on the petition. The others had not been notified of their status as defendants and were not represented by counsel. Hours later the court issued an injunction but limited it to the persons named in the board's initial motion. Other defendants could be added later. A few days later they were, but only after another lengthy dispute over the question of whether the board or the teachers' association was responsible for providing the court with a list of the names of education-association members. What the teachers won by all of this was (a) some precious hours of delay that were used to exert pressure on the board, and (b) a temporary limitation on the number of people affected by the court's initial injunctive order. The limitation meant that for several days rank-and-file teachers (as distinct from the named defendants) were not subject to the court's injunction, and to that extent, they were free to continue their strike.

Another common jurisdictional issue raised by teachers focuses on the courts' jurisdiction over the subject matter of a teacher–board labor dispute. In a 1978 California strike the teachers' attorney contended that the court did not have jurisdiction because the legislature had established a Public Employment Relations Board to consider charges of unfair labor practices (such as strikes); the PERB, not the local school board, was said to be the appropriate party to seek injunctive relief once the need for such relief had been established. While the argument was fruitless in this particular strike, the California Supreme Court soon thereafter accepted the same argument in a case growing out of a San Diego strike.[2] A similar issue has been advanced in Washington. A teacher attorney in

Washington acknowledged that as a practical matter, PERB jurisdiction would hardly preclude strikes, as the PERB was so understaffed that many months would elapse between the filing of a complaint and investigation of it. But of course that was not the point. The point was to remove the trial courts from the business of granting school-board requests for injunctive relief or possibly to encourage the court to play a PERB-like role in considering allegations of unfair labor practices in the context of injunction proceedings.

While jurisdictional challenges by teacher respondents rarely produce the type of legal victory exemplified by the San Diego case, they often do serve to make things more difficult for petitioners and to provide occasions for delaying tactics. It is other issues—particularly those relating to traditional restraints on the exercise of the courts' equitable powers—that provide the most fertile grounds for teacher defenses against injunction petitions.

Legality of Strikes

Equitable remedies are available only to protect interests recognized by law. Injunctions in early private-sector strikes were based on constitutional and statutory language that establish legally protected interests such as property or safety. However, in the case of teacher strikes there is not always clear language establishing that school boards have a legal right to be free of strikes or that teacher strikes are illegal. In the states whose statutes are silent, teacher attorneys advance elaborate arguments attempting to persuade the court that teacher strikes are not illegal. For example, in an extensive legal memorandum, attorneys for teachers in the 1978 Seattle strike noted that prohibition of strikes was a matter for legislative determination rather than court determination. The memorandum noted that the legislature was cognizant of the fact that there had been teacher strikes in Washington. It further noted that though strikes by certain categories of public employees had been expressly prohibited by statute, the legislature had defeated bills prohibiting strikes by teachers. The state board of education had even adopted rules defining a teacher strike and making provisions for establishing whether a school program was eligible for state reimbursement during a strike. To that extent, at least, the state had indicated willingness to countenance teacher strikes.[3] The petitioners, of course, had a different view and cited different authorities in support of it. The point is that the issue was joined, requiring the expenditure of time and effort on both sides and eventually forcing a judicial ruling.

Even in the states with explicit statutory provisions establishing that teacher strikes are illegal, diligent teacher attorneys can find opportunities to raise questions that may serve to delay proceedings. For example, if large numbers of teachers simultaneously take a day of personal leave, does it constitute a form of concerted activity tantamount to a strike? A Delaware court held that it did.[4] In another case the courts had to rule whether teacher refusal to attend a parents' night constituted a strike.[5] In situations in which a school board refuses to open school in the absence of a contract settlement, is there a strike? Pennsylvania teacher attorneys sometimes argue that such situations are lockouts, not strikes, and hence not proper matters for injunctions against teachers. However, these definitional defenses rarely arise. Strikes are hard to disguise. If a judge believes that a strike is in progress, and if there is no statutory prohibition against it, the judge can cite verities such as "public policy," "sovereignty," or the "duty to educate" as bases for establishing a strike's illegality. Nonetheless, by raising the issue, teacher attorneys may have rallied the strikers' morale and possibly generated some public sympathy for teachers who are denied rights granted to other categories of workers. And they may have won time, even if it is only the time required for the court to hear the argument.

In the states with limited right-to-strike laws, the question of a strike's illegality is a real issue. Typically the statutes provide that a strike is legal (a) if it occurs after all mandated impasse-resolution procedures have been exhausted and (b) until such time as the strike presents a clear and present danger to the public health or safety. It appears that the first condition usually is fairly easy to establish. The second is not, but we will reserve discussion of it to a later section on irreparable harm.

Availability of Alternate Forms of Relief

Another traditional limitation on equity cases has been that equitable relief will not be granted in the event that other forms of legal recourse are available. In some situations teacher attorneys engage in bluffing with this argument. For example, in an Illinois case the teachers' attorney contended that the board did not exhaust its remedies, inasmuch as there was a surplus of teachers in the state and the board could have hired some of them to replace the striking teachers.[6] Obviously, the strikers did not want this to happen, and their attorney probably would not have suggested it if he entertained any expectation that the board might initiate such an activity. The point, we suspect, was to buy more time, or possibly to induce the judge to think of ways to facilitate a settlement without so drastic a remedy. (The court later ordered daily negotiations sessions.)

Irreparable Harm

Teachers' attorneys argue that even if a teacher strike clearly is illegal, and even if there are no alternative remedies available to a board of education, the strike is not necessarily enjoinable, for there are further limitations on the courts' equitable powers. One of the most venerable of these is the irreparable harm standard: Injunctive relief may not issue unless its absence would result in irreparable harm to the petitioner. Until the 1968 *Holland* ruling in Michigan, courts routinely ignored the standard. But in *Holland* the court held that traditional equitable standards are applicable.[7] A Michigan attorney explains the significance of the decision in these terms:

> If we have any fighting chance to stop an . . . injunction . . ., it's on irreparable injury. That's all we ever put any weight on. Now many courts don't even listen to you on that because some statutes specifically say the strike may be enjoined. And if the statute says that, the court says the equitable prerequisites are not necessary. But if it doesn't say that, yes we do go in and we argue irreparable harm. . . . School boards never put any weight on it. Absolutely never. They get a superintendent to say the kids are losing some time and that's it. . . . We put in a lot of evidence.

An initial problem, of course, is to persuade a court that the irreparable harm standard is applicable. *Holland*-type appellate cases in Rhode Island, New Hampshire, and Wisconsin have eased the problem for teacher attorneys by opening the door to irreparable harm arguments.[8] In the states with limited right-to-strike laws, an analogous standard—danger to the public health, safety, or welfare—is available for use by teacher attorneys. Elsewhere, however, teacher attorneys have to urge the courts to apply the standard. Usually the effort is fruitless. A teacher attorney in New York explains that while the Taylor Act requires school boards to seek injunctive relief in the event of a strike, it does not require courts to grant the relief. But they routinely grant the relief by citing the illegality of strikes, and to date, the attorney laments, appeals have not yielded a *Holland*-type decision. In the state of Washington, where the statutes say nothing about the injunctive relief from teacher strikes, teachers' attorneys typically submit elaborate legal memoranda drawing the courts' attention to the *Holland* reasoning; in addition, affidavits are submitted contending that a strike is not harmful. But most Washington courts thus far have declined to consider the teachers' arguments.

At first glance, it seems odd that teachers would want to invoke the irreparable-harm standard. As one attorney notes, "It's kind of a dilemma. . . . We put in evidence showing [that] teachers are irrelevant. . . ." Perhaps it is this dilemma that explains the fact that in two California strikes, teachers did not respond to board allegations about the harm wrought by a strike; the teachers' challenges to injunctive relief rested on other grounds.

However, in several states where the courts do utilize the irreparable harm standard, teachers have found ways to avoid the dilemma of arguing that teachers are irrelevant. The teachers are rescued in part by the fact that the burden of proof is on the petitioners, who must show that irreparable harm will ensue if injunctive relief is not granted. Thus the teachers can insist that petitioners meet strict standards of proof in supporting their allegations of harm. Board witnesses are rigorously cross-examined. A Pennsylvania hearing illustrated how cross-examination can undermine a school board's allegations. In the following excerpt from the trial-court record, the teachers' attorney is cross-examining an assistant superintendent who had testified in support of the school board's allegation that seniors were being adversely affected by the strike because "absence from school creates a disadvantage to those required to take Scholastic Aptitude Exams and Achievement Tests and American College Tests."

Q. You stated yesterday that the seniors might experience some disadvantage because of the fact that they are not now in school because of the work stoppage, and they are about to take this ACT or SAT examination. . . . Can you tell us what disadvantages you are thinking about or referring to?

A: Yes, the disadvantage would be related to the interruption, the fact that the student is not currently attending classes. . . .

Q: Now, do you have some major, some empirical data that you could share with this court that would show that the mere interruption of the education from January 9 to this date would create such a disadvantage to these seniors?

A: I could not cite for you certain pieces of research, no.

Q: Upon what, then, sir, do you base your statement to this court?

A: My experience in working with learners in the classroom.

Q: All right. Let's explore that for a moment. What period of time can you tell this court, or what example can you tell this court where there had been a break in education for nine or ten days prior to an examination such as the SAT or the ACT which had caused some disadvantage to the person or persons to be tested?

A: I would correlate this with a teacher-made test, and if the learner had been absent for a period of time, even due to illness or Christmas vacation.

Q: [No,] I'm looking [for] similar tests so we can compare apples with

apples . . . not SAT to a history exam. . . . What examples would
you have for us?

A: In my opinion, the responsibilities and pressures placed upon a
youngster preparing for such an examination, and thinking in terms of
the value and future commitment of that student, this pressure in itself
for the SAT would increase the anxiety level. Now, if—

Q: Upon what do you base that; what example? My question has been
examples, sir.

A: My children taking such examinations; my own personal experience
in taking such examinations.

Q: So, that's one for you, and how many for the children now?

A: Pardon?

Q: How many children do you have?

A: Six.

Q: And they have all taken these examinations?

A: I believe my youngest daughter, the ACT, not the PSAT or SAT.

Q: So, you're speaking now of two personal experiences on these
examinations?

A: Not just two pesonal experiences. The students within our schools;
the comments made to me.

Q: Wait . . . let's take it, if we can, by the numbers here. You talked
about personal experience. You talked about yourself. All right?

A: Yes.

Q: Did you take the examination after being off for ten days because
of a work stoppage, as a student?

A: No, sir.

Q: So that doesn't count. How about your daughter, did she take the
examination coming off of a work stoppage?

A: No, sir.

Q: All right. Now, what other examples do you have?

A: I do not have any other examples.[9]

Later, in an interview, the same attorney indicated that such cross-examination was in some respects an exercise in futility.

No matter how skillful we have been in cross-examination, showing that
the specific harm that's been protrayed to us by their witnesses really
is not that harmful upon close scrutiny . . ., this seems not to be

impressive at all to the judge listening to the case. Almost as if it's a formality—that he's taking all this down for dress as opposed to any substance. No matter what we would say in counter-distinction, they will grant the injunction.

On the other hand, this attorney feels it is necessary to go through the motions—not merely because it buys precious time for the teachers but also because some day there might be an appeal on which the record would be useful.

Teacher attorneys find board allegations of harm unpersuasive. One attorney, for example, assesses the significance of allegations that strikes threaten state aid:

> One of the big allegations as to irreparable injury . . . in these suits is that if the teachers are not in their schools and the children are not there, that the school district will lose a lot of state aid. The basis for state aid for a district is the number of pupils that you have in attendance. Now . . . the fact remains that no school district has ever lost a penny as a result of a teachers' strike because of that count. What normally happens is the legislature simply passes a separate act that says the school district shall not lose any money as a result [of a strike]. There's a general feeling: why should it affect these kids and the school district and why should taxpayers lose money as a result of something over which they had absolutely no control? . . . Now there have been a couple of instances where in essence the school districts say, "Well, we just don't want to make the time up, so we'll just take the loss of state aid."

In courtroom proceedings, the teachers' point is made in a variety of ways. Through cross-examination of board witnesses or through testimony introduced by their own witnesses, teacher attorneys contend that state aid will not be lost if the school board has closed the schools since make-up days can be scheduled. If the board has elected to keep the schools open, and attendance is low, the responsibility is that of the board, not the teachers. Records of state-aid payments are introduced to support the point that state aid has not been forfeited in prior strikes.

Teacher respondents find arguments about pedagogical harm similarly unpersuasive. As a Washington attorney puts it, "I'm absolutely persuaded that these beginning-of-the-year strikes . . . cause absolutely no harm to anybody." Teacher affidavits were used to support such a contention in a Seattle strike. A math teacher declared:

> In 1976, teachers were on strike for approximately two weeks. Lost time occasioned by this delay in the opening of the school was made up during an extended school year. . . . In my judgment, and from my observations, that strike caused no irreparable harm to the mathematics program or to the education programs in general.[10]

In some cases teachers summon their own expert witnesses to argue that strikes do not cause irreparable harm. In one case the teachers' expert witness cited research studies indicating the absence of adverse effects from a strike, noted that scheduling of make-up days on Saturdays might be inconvenient but would not likely be harmful in view of the common practice of having Saturday classes in Europe and Japan, and stated that universities regularly made adjustments for summer-school students whose school year had been extended.

In addition to disputing the question as to whether there is harm, teacher attorneys frequently find it useful to admit that a strike may create harm and then to argue the issue as to how long a strike must last before the harm becomes irreparable. If teacher attorneys succeed in opening the door to discussion of *when* a strike becomes irreparably harmful, they then can introduce all sorts of arguments. Most of them focus on the school calendar. One of the unique features of teacher strikes in that they occur in an organization whose work days can be rescheduled. In Pennsylvania and Michigan the courts typically will not enjoin a strike until the time at which it is no longer possible to reschedule missed school days. Transcripts of injunction proceedings in Pennsylvania include long sections of argument in which the contending attorneys dispute the precise point at which this occurs. Should Saturdays be considered? If students are required to give up spring vacations or the early portions of their summer vacations, are the students irreparably harmed? In one case the teachers' attorney developed an elaborate argument in which he attempted to show that it was possible to define the school year in terms of instructional *hours,* and that by elongating the school day, it would be possible to schedule the requisite number of hours in less than 180 days. Such arguments prolong proceedings and force the court to make judgments that are admittedly arbitrary and that, therefore may serve to encourage the court to seek ways of settling the strike without having to resolve the calendar issues.

In Vermont where the statutes indicate that strikes can be enjoined when they present a "clear and present danger" to a "sound program of education," teacher attorneys succeeded in forestalling issuance of a preliminary injunction by arguing, in part, that while a strike interrupted a sound program of education, the danger was not clear and present until such time as the interrupted days could no longer be rescheduled.

Clean Hands

Teacher respondents often invoke the ancient equitable maxim that "He who seeks equity must come with clean hands." In the context of labor disputes the maxim suggests that school-board petitioners must have acted fairly in their dealings with teachers or, in the parlance of labor relations, engaged in "good-faith bargaining." Teacher respondents in an injunction proceeding often try to direct the court's attention to the allegedly "unclean hands" of the petitioner, in hopes that such action may induce the court to order good-faith bargaining, or even to withhold injunctive relief.

Reliance on the clean-hands defense was particularly significant in a strike in Everett, Washington. There the teacher respondents, using a combination of legal memoranda and affidavits from members of their bargaining team, stressed the theme that the board had failed to engage in good-faith bargaining and that "the District is only attempting to use this court as a lever in the course of its unfair labor practices." A detailed affidavit submitted by a teacher member of the bargaining team reviewed the past history of labor relations in the district, paying particular attention to prior litigation in which teachers had entered successful legal challenges to board labor practices. The affidavit went on to a day-by-day account of efforts to negotiate a new 1978–1979 contract. In a summary section the affidavit read as follows:

> Of the most concern . . . is the District's absolute refusal to bargain. They have constantly taken the position of an all-or-nothing offer and have even refused to address our proposal. The association negotiators have been put in an untenable position of countering its own counter-proposals. The board is remaining intransigent. The board has attempted everything to beat the bargaining process and to deal directly with members of our unit. The board has failed to provide information necessary to bargaining. . . .[11]

Specific incidents were cited in support of these and similar allegations. The board, of course, had its own complaints about unfair bargaining. However, the teachers' goal was to establish in the eyes of the court the idea that it should exercise discretion in the award of injunctive relief and that it "should not favor a governmental plaintiff which has not done equity." The court, the teachers suggested, "should strive to remain neutral as such neutrality will actually serve to encourage constructive settlement of such disputes." Apparently, the teachers' arguments carried some weight with the court, for the judge issued an interim order directing the parties to engage in at least ten hours of negotiations over the ensuing two days. The court also directed the federal mediator to report privately to the court as to whether the bargaining was in good faith. A ruling on injunctive relief was delayed. Later, when the injunction finally was issued, the judge again acknowledged the teachers' contentions, stating:

> I am convinced more and more as I listen to argument . . . that I should

in a supplemental order involve the courts to some degree in a monitoring of bargaining where the issues of bad faith or good faith can be reviewed by the court. . . . While the court is not particularly anxious to engage in that kind of work, I may find myself forced to, and . . . I'll certainly consider any order that either party should propose along that line, whether we call it a settlement conference or something else.[12]

A week later the teachers did ask the court to reenter the picture. The court appointed a fact-finder whose subsequent report provided the basis for a settlement. Here then the teachers' arguments on the clean-hands issue, while not sufficient to ward off an injunction, clearly did affect the nature of the court's remedial actions.

Teachers in an Illinois district pursued much the same tactic. Contending that the board was refusing to bargain, the teachers elicited an order directing daily negotiations over the Labor Day weekend—to the considerable distress of the board of education members who served on the negotiating team. After the Labor Day weekend, the attorneys reported back to the court: The negotiations had not been successful. The teachers contended that they had not been successful because they had not been taken seriously. One board member, the teachers told the court, arrived at a session with a six-pack of beer and one session was consumed almost entirely by a lengthy dinner meeting by the board. Perhaps, the teachers suggested, binding arbitration should be ordered by the judge. It was not, and the judge later enjoined the strike. But he moved slowly, repeatedly granting delays requested by the teachers. Meanwhile pressure was building on the board, and a settlement was reached just as contempt proceedings were launched.

The clean-hands argument then, like the irreparable-harm argument, sometimes serves to delay the issuance of injunctive relief. It has the further advantage—from the teachers' perspective—of eliciting judicial pressures to order a resumption of negotiations. Often such pressures precipitates board complaints about judicial meddling and court tyranny. However, we encountered one strike in which it appears that judicial pressure provided the board with a convenient and face-saving pretext for resuming negotiations that had collapsed over some name calling at the bargaining table.

Balancing the Equities

Another equitable principle occasionally invoked by teachers rests on the concept of fairness. Here the court must ask whether issuance of an injunction to protect the petitioners' interests might create even worse harm to the respondents. In Washington a teacher attorney reports:

I'm persuaded by the affidavits that we've gotten from the educational psychologists and the counselors who say that far more harm is caused to the educational process by requiring a school to start with teachers under an injunction who don't know what their pay is going to be. . . . They know that their bargaining power has been destroyed and that they're going to come out with less than they could have gotten if they'd been allowed to strike for a couple of weeks. And so morale is down. Not much is happening in the classroom.

Affidavits making the point were submitted to the court. One teacher declared:

Forcing teachers to go back to school before there is resolution and mutual agreement means that the school staff would be working under more than the usual opening-of-school stress. When people are under stress, it is reflected in increases in interpersonal conflicts . . . and inability to see others' views. It may also lead to apathetic task performance. If we increase stress and anxiety on school staff, we in turn decrease their ability to be responsive to students' needs, interests, and tensions.[13]

We found little evidence to indicate that such statements affect judicial decisions to issue or not issue injunctive relief. An exception occurred in a Vermont strike where teachers relied heavily on this theme. There a temporary restraining order had been issued, and teachers had returned to work. At the hearing on a request for a preliminary injunction, teachers testified that such an order would be demoralizing to them. It would also diminish the likelihood that an acceptable settlement could be negotiated inasmuch as the board then would have an unfair advantage if a new strike could not be called.[14] On the basis of this and other arguments, the preliminary injunction was not issued.

In strikes in Springfield (Illinois) and Washington, D.C., judicial cognizance of basic equitable balance led to injunctions that were accompanied by court orders to reinstitute expired contracts; this at least assured the teachers of having some contractual basis for salary and working conditions.[15] There too, then, teachers found some benefits in the injunctive process.

Sanctions

Despite the teachers' efforts to head them off, injunctions were issued sooner or later in 71 percent of the cases in which they were sought during 1978–1979 teacher strikes. Teachers complied with one-third of the back-to-work orders. In a few cases it appears that compliance occurred because an injunction provided a face-saving pretext for ending a strike that was collapsing anyway. However, in other cases the collapse was itself fostered by the injunction. An injunction is, after all, a powerful device. Those who defy an injunction risk personal fines and jail sentences; teacher organizations risk seizure of their assets and future dues. There also are powerful social norms of law-abidingness that an injunction activates. Heroic statements of defiance notwithstanding, many teachers are unwilling to defy the law and accept the consequences. A Pennsylvania attorney, explaining why an injunction ended a strike, points out:

> These people had been exhausted, I believe, and the public ostracism of having a member of the family being placed in jail by violating a lawful court order was enough to persuade them to capitulate.

An organization president in Michigan notes:

> There was always someone sitting out there saying, "But I have a moral responsibility to not break the law." There are some people who just absolutely can't face that. They don't relate at all to the concept of civil disobedience.

But compliance is the exception. Two-thirds of the 1978–1979 back-to-work orders were defied by teachers. Defiance occurs for a variety of reasons. Many teacher leaders believe that defiance of an injunction is necessary in order to shift attention to the underlying teacher–board dispute. Put differently, they believe it necessary to demonstrate that they can absorb judicial sanctions in order to persuade the board of education or the court that negotiations, not injunctions, are required to end the strike. A national organizer puts it this way:

> Most of the boards with whom we deal aren't prepared to alter their positions until after they utilize the weapons they have—injunctions, fines, jailing, and whatever follows . . . and see how we react. . . . Finally, we get to the point where they take us seriously and we start some bargaining.

A teacher official in Michigan describes how defiance of an injunction helped achieve a resumption of negotiations:

> The governor of the state . . . started getting pressure to do something because it was obvious that we had indeed broken the injunction and now were really putting the school system into a threatening situation. He couldn't just sit there. . . . So he appointed . . . [a] fact-finder [who] . . . is considered to be somewhat prolabor.

A teacher-association president in California also indicates that defiance of an injunction was a key to getting the board to negotiate:

> I don't believe that the reality of the situation really hit that school board until they started serving [summons upon] the teachers finally. And no one did anything. No one cared. They were willing to go to jail. . . . So I think the school board recognized: What are you going to do? Are you going to put three hundred teachers in jail? What will that serve? Because we would stay there. We would still have the right to negotiate.

In the 1978 Bridgeport strike, 265 teachers—one-fifth of the total teaching force in the city—were jailed and fines amounting to more than $900,000 were levied. The teachers did not reduce their demands in the face of these sanctions. Neither did the board. In the end it took an arbitrated settlement to end the strike.[16]

Another reason for defying injunctions is that defiance can strengthen the solidarity and the resolve of striking teachers. Jailed teachers become martyrs in the eyes of their fellow teachers, helping to sustain strike morale and solidarity. One Pennsylvania teacher attorney speaks of the positive effects of his unsuccessful efforts to bail out jailed teacher leaders:

> The judge, contrary to his promise to me, denied them bail. I went to seven courts in six days and lost every one of them. . . . Every state court and every federal court. But the troops were really up in arms. It gave them such a spirit. [It was] such a morale booster. Every day I lost, and the headlines were there. And they paraded around the prison 4,000 strong on Sunday. . . . [demonstrating] spirit and morale.

Much the same phenomenon was evident in the Bridgeport strike, where, according to a local press report, morale was high among teachers jailed at a National Guard camp. "Thousands" of New England teachers reportedly staged a sympathy rally outside the camp gates.[17] Later reports indicated that the jailed teachers were bored and tense but exhibited no weakening of resolve.[18] An attorney describes the psychology of the phenomenon: "You can't force a guy to go back to work. They arch their back and they say, 'I'll see the inside of the slammer first.' "

There is still another rationale behind willingness to accept penalties. It helps neutralize claims that teachers are setting a bad example to children by violating antistrike laws. Incarceration can be linked to the tradition of civil disobedience. One teacher attorney reports:

> I had a black superintendent on the stand . . . asking him what the image of Martin Luther King being dragged away to jail was on black students, and he thought that was a very good image.

A teacher leader engaged in a long monologue about the phenomenon, contending that the right to strike was fundamental and hard won and that teachers who invoked that right in their own behalf were teaching an important lesson in civics, particularly insofar as the teachers were willing to pay the penalties traditionally associated with civil disobedience.

Despite the brave rhetoric, sanctions are not viewed casually. A teacher organization president in a Western state has this to say about her immediate response to an injunction naming her:

> The weight of the office hit me. I mean I was aware of the gravity and realized the consequences of violating, what could happen. . . . I know people who have been in jail for teacher strikes. And there isn't one of them . . . who won't tell you that it's a terrible experience. Just because it never happened in this state doesn't mean it couldn't. So, yeh, I was a little nervous.

Fines also can be damaging. As one leader points out:

> You can always serve the jail time, but the fines hang on and on and on. I guess the part that I was worried about more than anything else was the fines. . . . Because I have seen organizations almost put out of business by those fines.

A variety of devices are used to delay the imposition of sanctions, to reduce their likelihood, and to lessen their magnitude. Many of these tactics do not involve injunction proceedings directly. For example, one person describes how the prospect of jailing can be thwarted:

> And there's neat ways of handling it. You know, you throw the president in jail. The vice president comes up. He refuses to say "Go back." So they throw him in jail. They do that several times. And eventually the teachers are going . . . to elect the nicest, oldest schoolteacher in the district who's raised and taught half the children. . . .

In the 1979 Saint Louis strike teacher-organization officials were very much aware that their president—a black woman—was not likely to be prosecuted for contemp by a predominantly white school board in a city where a majority of the teachers and students were black and where other race-related issues were simmering. The president's reported willingness to go to jail was an important piece of the strike gamesmanship and may have been a factor in the court's noticeable aversion to expediting injunction proceedings.

Inside the courtroom all manner of legal maneuvers are used to resist the imposition of sanctions. Inquiries may be made as to whether alleged contemnors received proper notice of the actions enjoined. Efforts may be made to secure a jury trial if the charges are for criminal contempt. If negotiations are under way, there may be efforts to delay contempt proceedings so that negotiations may continue—particularly if those accused of contempt also are members of the teachers' bargaining team. Often the actual calculation and imposition of fines is delayed until after the strike itself is ended. By this point, of course, the petitioners have very little interest in prosecuting the matter, inasmuch as such prosecution can hardly restore productive working conditions in the schools.

On the Line

Courtroom proceedings are, by design, insulated from the social disputes that precipitate litigation. However, strike organizers typically take steps to assure that rank-and-file teachers are not completely isolated from courtroom events. Some information is disseminated in order to reduce the risk that teachers will be surprised or worried by injunction proceedings. For example, a bulletin passed out to teachers prior to a strike vote in Saint Louis contains the following:

Q: Isn't it against the law to strike?

A: No! But the board can go to court and seek an injunction against employees striking. This injunction usually is granted by the judge. Striking employees are then in violation of a court injunction if they refuse to return to work.

Q: Can I be served with an injunction?

A: Yes, and you probably will be. When you are served with yours, immediately turn it over to your picket captain who is under instructions to promptly forward it to our strike coordinator [who] has arranged for the union's attorneys to handle it from there.

Q: Is is true that teachers . . . have been fined for remaining on strike?

A: Yes, but it is also true that no such striker in any AFT strike has ever had to pay that fine out of his/her own pocket.

Q: Is it true that teachers . . . have been jailed for remaining on strike?

A: Yes! Boards of education often sit back and do nothing until they see if that tactic will succeed in terrorizing their striking employees into a back-to-work stampede or at least a gradual erosion of support. This board tactic has been unsuccessful in those strikes in which the employees have willingly gone to jail with full intention to remain there for the duration of the strike. When the board found that they couldn't have the teachers . . . in school and in jail at the same time, a fair settlement soon followed.

Injunction proceedings also are reported at carefully staged rallies where solidarity and righteousness are nourished, where the presence of colleagues can reduce fear, and where the court action is offered as one more instance of the bad motives of the board. The same theme is presented in bulletins to picketing teachers, as in this bulletin:

> We warned you that the board would seek injunctions in the courts to attempt to force you back to work. It has happened. The restraining order has been issued. . . . We cannot give up our fight now. This is a board tactic to break our strike. There is only one solution . . . we must show our strength. If necessary, we'll pack the jails. We cannot return to work until we have a ratified settlement and a contract that we can be proud of. If we stand together, we will win this war.

But the outcome of the "war" is not entirely within the control of teachers. The action and decision of the judge may deprive them of their victory.

Notes

1. Robert G. Stabile, *Anatomy of Two Teacher Strikes* (Cleveland: EduPress Publishing, 1974).

2. *San Diego Teachers Association v. Superior Court,* 154 Cal. Rptr. 893, Cal. Sup. Ct. (1979).

3. Defendants' Memorandum in Opposition to Motion for Peliminary Injunction, *Seattle School District No. 1 v. Seattle Teachers' Association,* No. 851172, King County Super. Ct., Wash. (September 25, 1978).

4. *State of Delaware v. Delaware State Educational Association,* 326 A.2d. 868 Del. Ch. (1974).

5. *The Yearbook of School Law, 1977* (Topeka: National Organization on Legal Problems in Education, 1977), p. 242.

6. David L. Colton, "A Teacher Strike in Collinsville, Illinois," mimeographed (Saint Louis: Center for the Study of Law in Education, Washington University, 1980).

7. *School District for the City of Holland v. Holland Education Association,* 157 N.W.2d. 206, Mich. Sup. Ct., (1968).

8. *School Committee of Westerly v. Westerly Teachers' Association,* 299 A.2d. 441, Sup. Ct. of R.I. (1973); *Timberlane Regional School District v. Timberlane Regional Education Association,* 317 A.2d. 555 (1974); and *Joint School District No. 1 v. Wisconsin Rapids Education Association,* 234 N.W.2d. 289, Wis. Sup. Ct. (1975).

9. Transcript of Proceedings, *Butler Area School District v. Penn-*

sylvania State Education Association et al., Equity No. 78–002, Ct. of Common Pleas, Butler County, Pa. (January 20, 1978).

10. Affidavit of Robert Probach, *Seattle School District No. 1 v. Seattle Teachers' Association*, No. 851172, King County Super. Ct., Wash. (September 6, 1978).

11. Affidavit of Michael Wartelle in Opposition to Plaintiffs' Motion for Temporary Restraining Order and Injunctive Relief, *Everett School District No. 2 v. Everett Education Association*, No. 78–2–02952–1, Super. Ct., Snohomish County, Wash. (September 19, 1978).

12. Oral Ruling of the Court, *Everett*, p. 6.

13. Affidavit of Floyd Hammersla, *Seattle*.

14. Transcript of Proceedings, *Board of School Commissioners of the City of Rutland and Rutland School District v. Rutland Education Association*, No. S371–79Rc, Rutland Super. Ct., Vt. (January 11, 1980).

15. Temporary Restraining Order, *Board of Education of Springfield Public Schools District No. 186 v. Springfield Education Association*, No. 486–76, Circuit Ct. Seventh, Sangamon County, Ill. (August 31, 1976); and Memorandum Opinion and Order, *Vincent Reed et al., v. Washington Teachers' Union*, C.A. No. 2534–79, Super. Ct. of the District of Columbia (March 28, 1979).

16. *Bridgeport* (Conn.) *Post*, September 25, 1978.

17. *Hartford Courant*, September 14 and September 18, 1978.

18. *Bridgeport* (Conn.) *Post*, September 22, 1978.

6 Judges as Decision Makers

The complaint or petition for injunctive relief that the board brings before the judge focuses on only one aspect of the original dispute between boards and teachers. The extent to which the judge perceives and takes judicial notice of the wider collective-bargaining dispute, of the positions and interests of the parties, and of the efficacy of judicial remedies to ameliorate and resolve the dispute may affect how the court responds to the petition before it.

We have noted the broad scope of the powers of a judge in an injunction proceeding. One judge notes the awesome responsibility that is the court's:

> An injunction is the exercise of an extraordinary power by the judicial branch of the government; and it is the only situation in our governmental scheme and constitutional scheme where one man, a judge, can pass a law you might say, for a particular case, and then on his own punish people for violating that law, including jail time and fines. And, further than that, even if a court finds later or determines that the judge was wrong in issuing the injunction in the first place, [that] does not excuse the violator . . . so the court in approaching this does it with a lot of care and caution.[1]

In order to understand the dilemma in which judges are placed in these cases, we will examine what judges do and what judges say about their role in teacher-strike injunction cases.

What Judges Do

Among the districts that experienced teacher strikes in 1978–1979, about 40 percent filed petitions for injunctive relief. Our survey of strikes included responses from fifty-one districts that sought help from the court. We can trace four patterns of judicial response to the petitions of boards.

First, judges usually grant relief to school boards. Among the fifty-one petitioners, thirty-six (71 percent) received orders restricting the teachers' strike activities. Boards that initially sought relief on an *ex parte* basis reported higher success rates than boards that participated in show cause hearings. Of the twenty-two districts that filed for *ex parte* relief,

77 percent (seventeen of twenty-two) received favorable judicial rulings. (Two others obtained relief after a show cause hearing, bringing the success rate for these twenty-two districts to 86 percent.) Among the twenty-nine districts where show cause hearings preceded initial court rulings, the petitioners' success rate was lower—59 percent.

A second pattern of judicial response was to become engaged in efforts to promote settlement of the underlying dispute. Half of all injunction proceedings produced judicial orders directing the parties to engage in additional negotiations. Usually these directives coincided with rulings on the board's request for relief, but in nine cases the directives preceded the judicial decisions.

A third pattern was simply not to issue an order. Among the fifteen districts whose petitions were not approved, few had their requests explicitly denied by judges. The most common pattern was for injunction proceedings to move forward concurrently with settlement efforts (with or without judicial participation in such efforts); settlements were achieved before orders were issued.

Fourth, judges dealt with teacher noncompliance. We have noted that teachers complied with half of the orders restricting picketing but with only one-third of the orders mandating cessation of the strike or return to the classroom. Our data show that both boards and courts viewed the noncompliance with picketing orders as the less serious of the two. We found no instance in which teachers were either charged with or cited with contempt of court when their noncompliance was with picketing orders only.

But noncompliance with orders to cease striking or to return to work is a different matter. Of the twenty instances of noncompliance with such orders, boards authorized contempt motions in eighteen cases and filed such motions in sixteen. In eleven of these cases, the judge found teachers in contempt. In each case teachers were either fined or jailed; sometimes both occurred. A court may initiate contempt charges on its own motion if a board fails to do so. In four instances, judges initiated such proceedings. In all four cases, teachers were fined and in two, teachers were jailed.

In two contempt cases, the judge ordered the board to fire teachers who had been found in contempt of court. The superintendent of one of these districts reported that the judge "has taken under advisement damages (actual and punitive) because the board of education didn't fire 3,000 teachers." In this case, court action led to a remedy that the board had not anticipated and that it refused to implement, even when ordered to do so by the court.

In summary, judges issue injunctions, they direct parties to negotiate, they deny or simply fail to issue injunctions (for inaction is itself a response), and they adjudicate contempt charges. The outcomes of efforts to seek injunctive relief from teacher strikes are thus by no means uniform. We turn now to the task of understanding the varieties of judicial response.

Negotiations in Chambers

Much of the interesting and significant action in a teacher-strike case takes place in the chambers of the judge. It is here that the judge probes the positions of the parties and assesses the chances for informal settlement. But it is difficult to research these interactions since access is limited to those directly concerned. Still, from our interviews with parties, we have constructed a composite account of judicial action, using the direct words of the participants to report on how the judge attempted to resolve that particular strike. This report reveals that negotiation occurs not only between attorneys for the parties but also between the attorneys and the judge. And the negotiation involves not only the legal dispute but also the underlying bargaining dispute.

The following account is based on a strike that occurred in 1978–1979. A temporary restraining order was granted *ex parte*. A date for a show cause hearing was set ten days thereafter.

A Case Study

Board attorney: It's difficult . . . to have any real control over the timing. You're pretty much at the mercy of the court. The court pretty much controls that. You know, typically the teachers' union wants to delay just as long as possible. And they will use any tactic they can. Typically, those seeking the injunction want to push it as fast as possible. And the judge pretty much sets the tone by his willingness or unwillingness to hear evidence.

Teacher-organization leader: I really have a lot of respect for the judge in that I really think he sized up this situation just about like it was. He saw that . . . we did have reasons to grieve and that we had no legitimate way to do it. And here, the people who were perpetrating the grievous situations on us simply were doing us [sic] anyway they wanted to and . . . they would use the law to punish us. And we really were boxed in and so what he did was simply not be used or rushed into anything. (**Q:** And he delayed ten days?) The whole thing was, though, in those ten days he really gave us a chance to communicate and resolve and get out of the situation.

Board attorney: (**Q:** The judge did not appear to be in any great haste to apply the law nor did he particularly seem enthused about his enforcement.) I have that same impression of judge X and had it as we were going along. But, on the other hand, these are terribly significant lawsuits, and naturally the judge wants to be very conscientious and accurate in his rulings. And so there's a natural tendency to go slow. I think though that in the background is also the feeling that an injunction is going to be ignored. It's going to make matters worse. "I know what my responsibilities ultimately are, but can't," you know, he says, "can't we get this thing settled so I don't have to take that hard approach and order the teachers to return?" In the first injunction suit this time around, Judge X was constantly asking the attorneys if there wasn't something that could be done to clarify the issues and hopefully resolve them. He was hoping against hope that the thing could be settled quickly so that he wouldn't have to make that tough decision. So I think that consideration causes a judge naturally to move more slowly than the school board wishes he would move. From our point of view, we would like him to move very quickly and decisively because we have the law on our side.

Second board attorney: Most of the initial proceedings were in chambers . . . the hours of discussion we had in chambers, just literally hours of discussion . . .

Teacher attorney: Parties appeared at the show cause hearing. At that time the court called the parties into conference and after some discussion ordered the parties to prepare a report defining the issues and at the same time urged the parties to meet together to solve their problems by discussions. . . . The court continued the case for approximately seven days. . . . Meetings began between the parties in an attempt to resolve their differences. These meetings continued until the matter was resolved.

Board attorney: (Commenting on the second court proceeding, a lengthy show cause hearing during which both parties agreed that attorneys for teachers used delaying tactics): Judge X had heard all the evidence and wanted to sit back and think about it and make his ruling the next Monday or Tuesday. And I said ". . . People are saying that the courts aren't giving anybody any support. The strike is illegal. You know it's illegal. We know it's illegal." You could tell from what he had been talking about the whole time back in chambers that he was going to enter the order. I said, "Come on, you know, give us our order." And so finally he said, "Well, come back tomorrow afternoon (which was Friday) about 3:30 or 4:00." But he said, "Don't bring the defendants or any of the people." He said, "We'll bring them in next Monday" so we brought them in Monday, then, and he gave them the order. . . . Well, by that time we all knew the strike was going to be over. It really broke that weekend I guess, in the negotiations.

In chambers, away from the formal procedures of the courtroom, the judge has an opportunity to explore the full range of issues and to assess the problems and positions of the parties. The remedy at hand, the injunction, may, in the eyes of the judge, simply not provide a good "fit" to the problem at hand. And the judge may be persuaded that there must surely be some way to get the parties together. In another 1978–1979 strike, the teacher-organization leader conveyed her perception of the position of the judge:

> I think his initial try, even though he might not have cognitively artic-
> ulated it in that fashion, was based on the good instincts which people
> who are basically problem-solvers have . . . they want to talk to the
> person who is responsible, who is in charge and sit down with them
> with the belief, not just the knowledge, but the absolute belief that you
> can come to agreement—that human beings can solve any problem
> that's of human origin.

It appears that only when the judge has tried to bring the parties together in a number of ways and becomes reluctantly persuaded of the intransigence of one party or both that he or she realizes that a decision cannot be avoided.

What Judges Say

Judges indicate that teacher-strike cases are difficult cases to process. In their comments in written and oral decisions, in writing for their legal peers or the broader public, in interviews, and in their practices in chambers (as revealed by comments of the parties to the dispute), some note that they do not enjoy adjudicating these cases. There are many factors in the circumstances surrounding these disputes that prompt judges to weigh very carefully the decision they render and, in some instances, even to avoid issuing a court order at all. As the judge surveys the facts of the case and the law that applies to those facts, he or she may discover that both are characterized by considerable complexity. And the dispute is situated in a societal context that makes the dispute highly visible, emotionally charged, and of an emergency nature; the effects of the strike intensify as additional days go by.

The Law and the Facts of the Case

Private-sector labor relations are governed by federal legislation facili-tating uniformity of rules across state boundaries, the more rapid build-up of applicable precedent, and the progressive removal of legal uncer-tainty. However, in the public sector, each state governs its own state and local cases; a number still have no relevant case law. But even within a state, wide variation remains. An order of a trial court is valid only for the judicial district in which it is issued; it does not have a statewide effect. Pennsylvania's limited right-to-strike law, for instance, spells out conditions under which strikes are permitted and under which they may be enjoined. A Pennsylvania judge notes that during the first three years under the act, there were 123 strikes.

> Of these, thirty were enjoined by the courts. A review of the cases reflects no consistency. This may be accounted for by the fact that there are sixty-seven autonomous jurisdictions in the Commonwealth of Pennsylvania. . . . This then lending itself to ad hoc determinations.[2]

If there is uncertainty where the statute is explicit, there is more where there are no statutory provisions on the rights of teachers to strike. Or the statute may be ambiguous. An appellate judge in Pennsylvania indicates:

> When legislatures finally determine to adopt a wholly new concept of public management, they usually do so in terms more expressive of their fear of the unforseeable harm which may result from the new policy than of their confidence in the good it will accomplish. Hence, such legislation is often tentative, imprecise, elliptical and incomplete, leaving the hard choices either to the improbable chance that they ''may not come up,'' or to the courts.[3]

Some judges feel ''put upon'' by the inaction of legislatures:

> [O]bviously this is an area that cries out for legislation. And at least so far as the court is concerned, it cries out for legislation because it would make our job easier if we knew what the public policy of the state was as applied to teachers' strikes. We have case law and other things . . . that talk about public employees' right to strike, . . . but the square issue of whether school teachers should have the right to strike has not been squarely met in this state, as far as I know at least, by either the legislature or . . . by the appellate courts. Everyone— teachers, administrators, students, parents, taxpayers, as well as courts—would have an easier job with these things if their rights and duties were spelled out.[4]

The legal rules are subject to varying interpretations, ambiguous or absent. The fact situation can also be complex. The case before the bench may be the first public-sector case the judge has heard and there may be little time to understand the issues of the case. Because of the emergency nature of strikes, injunction cases are normally handled with little delay, often within hours of the initial filing of the complaint. A Washington board attorney notes:

> You have to realize that the judge finds out about five minutes to nine

that he has this case, and at 9:00 or so, he's going through a stack of
material about five inches deep, trying to assimilate all of that information. Then he's listening to arguments and then he is ruling. And it
is not easy to comprehend all the legal issues and the factual issues
under those circumstances.

In adjudicating a teacher-strike case, the judge is entering another insti-
tutional world. There is much to assimilate. A Pennsylvania judge asserts:

> The authority vested in the court is unprecedented. . . ; the court is
> called upon to digest the economic, professional and managerial com-
> plexities of an educational system, assume problems unresolved by
> mediation and/or fact-finding commissions, and decide what is in the
> best interests of the public.[5]

External Political and Social Pressures

If the legal and fact situations facing the judge are complex, the social
context for the case is also much broader, more highly visible, and more
emotionally charged than is the usual civil case. These factors may encourage a judge to use judicial restraint, delay, or negotiation to resolve
the dispute. We examine first some of the external social and political
factors that a judge may weigh.

A Pennsylvania teacher attorney notes the high visibility given the
judge in some teacher-strike cases:

> There are two million people in Philadelphia. Maybe three quarters of
> a million or a million people are affected by the school shutdown—
> families, the children and everything else, including the teachers and
> their families. Therefore, what bigger case can a judge get in his court-
> room to help three-fourth of a million people? Whereas otherwise he's
> dealing with a criminal case and may only affect one person or, in a
> civil case, affect two.

Judges indicate that public opinion is often strong and volatile in
these cases. A trial-court judge asserts:

> Nothing has aroused the public so greatly in our forty-eight years upon
> the Common Pleas bench as the failure to provide to the thousands of
> students the education which the law provides for them.[6]

A Pennsylvania appellate judge notes the pressures facing the trial-court
judge in a teacher-strike case:

> Nothing written here is intended to be critical of the court below since

its role is a most difficult one. The words of the applicable statute and the reported pronouncements of the appellate courts on one side, and the exigencies of the situation that confronts him on the other side, make his moment of decision a most unenviable one. Being the parent of a child enrolled in a school district that as recently as September 1973 experienced the ordeal of a school strike, I am well cognizant of the many community pressures, added to the assertions of teacher and school board, that center on the chancellor.[7]

The difficulty of such cases is also noted by a Delaware trial court:

First, of course, courts do not enjoy getting involved in labor disputes. It is a difficult area of the law and the court has difficulty coming through such litigation without being scarred. But courts do not exist to avoid scars or complex problems. Courts exist to enforce the law. Simply because a judge or a group of judges think that a given problem could be better handled elsewhere is no basis for the court to avoid its responsibility to enforce existing law. Judges do not enjoy the luxury of choosing the litigation that is brought before their court.[8]

Teacher-strike cases may be not only highly visible but also highly political. They may be political, first of all, in the sense that political figures in the jurisdiction of the court (and even outside it) become involved. There have been numerous instances in recent teacher strikes in which local civic and religious leaders, the mayor of the city, and even the governor of the state became involved in public attempts to resolve the strike while it was pending in court.

The strike may also be political in the sense that covert political pressure is brought to bear on the judge to produce a certain outcome. A teacher-union leader in a northern state describes the channels used to persuade Judge A not to issue comtempt citations against teachers:

We had a lot of politics going on that weekend. The head of [a major labor union] talked to Judge B who was running for court of appeals and had formerly been a bench partner of Judge A. B, through the influence of the union, went to see Judge A that weekend to advise him not to come down with contempts [sic]. We had a judge who was running for probate judge, C. And in both cases, we were of course endorsing them after the strike and really did a lot for them. And they both won. But C happened to be a good friend of one of the teachers in one of the small districts on the east side of town. And he was best friends with A. And he went to see A on our behalf with the same advice.

A judge may or may not be influenced by such pressures. It is possible that Judge A would have arrived at a similar decision independently. However, such covert political pressures must be weighed along with legal factors in understanding the milieu in which judges issue (or do not issue) injunctions.

Finally, there may be political pressure of a third kind. Many trial-court judges are elected to office. Where a decision may alienate a significant segment of the community, it is good to have a clear and compelling legal reason on which to base that decision. And it is better to avoid widespread alienation if possible. The relationship between the decision of the judge and his assessment of his reelection chances is a complex one. Still our interviewees indicate at least one instance in which a judge handling a teacher-strike case was subsequently defeated for reelection; his ruling in the case was given as a major cause. Hence a judge may weigh his own position with voters as another factor in the context of decision to which he or she pays some heed. A Pennsylvania school-board attorney comments, ''Judges are political animals. That's how they got to be judges in the first place.''

In addition to strong public opinion and the exercise of political influence, the number of cases awaiting hearing may influence how a judge will handle a case. An *ex parte* request for an injunction means that the matter can be handled without a court hearing. Hence a judge may attempt to quickly handle the request for injunctive relief in this way. However, some states do not allow *ex parte* relief. If there is a crowded docket, a Missouri board attorney notes that the judge may then attempt to foster a settlement out of court, making it unnecesary for the court to rearrange its calendar in order to conduct a hearing. A Michigan state educator comments:

> In this state, judges know they can't issue an injunction right away unless they have a show cause hearing on irreparable harm. And so consequently, rather than go through all that . . . the judges have a tendency just to say, ''OK, I'll order extensive negotiations and you negotiate and come back.'' And politically, it's better for them.

Other Considerations

In addition to the external pressures of publicity, political factors, and the effect of the court docket, there are other considerations that determine how the judge will approach the case. Will he or she focus only on the precise legal issue that is before the court—the illegal strike? It is the formal issue that the board is urging the court to adjudicate. Or will the judge take into account the broader context in which the case is embedded?

The decision to focus and rule only on the issue of illegality has much to commend it. The long-range pressure on the judge is to rule against behavior that is prohibited by law. The judge's own training, the examples and opinions of peers, the pressure of community criticism, the insistence of petitioners charging unlawful action by respondents, and the strike situation that daily becomes more precarious and tense—all combine to promote an eventual issuance of an injunction in the majority of cases at some point.

Some judges issue the injunction immediately. Courts are most secure and can maintain the image of impartiality and justice best when they reason from a legal prohibition.[9] In such an instance the case requires nothing more than a determination of fact (whether a strike is taking place) and an application of law (that such strikes are illegal).

But a judge may have second thoughts. What does equity require in this case? What can be accomplished with issuing an order? With refraining from issuing an order? What if teachers do not obey the orders of the court? And what if the board chooses not to file contempt charges? Then the court is faced with a case of clear defiance of its orders by a significant segment of the community. What will be the result for the legitimacy of law and the credibility of the court? In what light will the judge be placed? True, the court has the power to institute contempt proceedings on its own. But this places the onus of action firmly on the shoulders of the judge. Is it necessary to become involved to that extent in a case whose ultimate resolution is clearly the responsibility of the parties that are before the court? Suppose the teachers go on striking after fines are levied against them for contempt; what then? Suppose the board negotiates an amnesty agreement with teachers in the eventual settlement and then petitions the court to revoke fines? Might these outcomes be prevented by denying an injunction, by refusing to issue an order, or by ordering the parties to return to the bargaining table?

The judge may also assess the effectiveness of the injunctive remedy. Will it resolve the dispute? Can it? One court asserts:

> Regardless of what this court decides, the real problem involved herein will be resolved only when the teachers and the school district commence renegotiations and enter into a contract.[10]

Another court notes that sanctions may be counterproductive:

> The question as to what sanctions should appropriately be imposed on public employees who engage in illegal strike activity is a complex one which, in itself raises significant issues of public policy. In the past, several states have attempted to deter public employee strikes by imposing mandatory, draconian statutory sanctions on striking employees; experience has all too frequently demonstrated, however, that such harsh, automatic sanctions do not prevent strikes but instead are counterproductive, exacerbating employer–employee friction and prolonging work stoppages.[11]

Thus, despite the gravity of the crisis, the judge may see that an injunction is an inappropriate solution for a collective-bargaining dispute. The injunction cannot resolve the outstanding issues between the parties. It cannot force the parties to bargain in good faith. It will not ameliorate the already strained and tense relationships between the parties.[12] Hence, even if there are sufficient grounds for issuing the injunction, it may be unwise to do so. One trial-court judge commented:

> Injunctions or temporary restraining orders . . . are addressed to the discretion of the court, and there are many instances where there may be a basis for the issuance of an injunction, but for whatever reason that remedy may not be a very practical one or a very good one under all the circumstances. In those cases I think it's appropriate for the court to exercise its discretion in whether to grant or not to grant an injunction.[13]

The court may also pay attention to the effect of an injunction, if issued, in weighting the subsequent bargaining process against one party or the other. Injunctions distribute power. By deciding for the board (or the teachers), the court lends the weight of law and the prestige of the courts to one party and against the other. A Pennsylvania judge notes the effects:

> If the court issues an injunction, it is unlikely that the demands of the public-school teacher will be met. Should the court refuse to grant the injunction, the public employer may capitulate to the demands. The public employer then blames the court for forcing it to agree to unreasonable demands by the union. Neither result is in the public interest. . . . A trial judge is placed by PERA (Public Employee Relations Act) in a position that is not only untenable but also one that requires more of a political and economic result than a judicial decision.[14]

Judges struggle with the power-distributive aspect of their decision (or nondecision). They may announce that what they decide is not to be seen in that light. One judge noted, "I don't want this ruling to be interpreted by anyone as favoring either the school district or the teachers on these negotiations."[15] Another judge denied that it was the business of the court to weight the bargaining process:

> The court does not act to interfere in the collective-bargaining process on one side or the other. The court enjoins a strike. Public employees have no legal right to strike and, if they are using the strike as part of the bargaining process, they are bargaining illegally. It is not even generally an answer to say that the public employer is violating the law in some respect.[16]

But whether a judge acknowledges it or not, a court order does alter the balance of power between the parties in bargaining. But then, so does refusing to grant an order. A course of action that may then commend itself to the judge may be to defer issuance of the order and to send the parties back to the bargaining table, using the prestige of the court and the threat of impending action against the party that does not bargain in good faith.

But for other judges with a pragmatic mind-set and a problem-solver approach, the goal of intervening in a strike is to adjudicate the matter neither in the interest of the board or the teachers but in the public interest. What their decision will do to the collective-bargaining issues in the case, directly or inadvertently, is for them not of significance. A judge in a northern state, who has recently adjudicated a teacher strike, explains:

> I don't think that's in a judge's mind at all, which side has the greatest power. The important thing is to get the strike settled. The important thing is to protect the public. . . . In a school strike, it is the public that is being hurt. Our function is to protect the public interest. And our aim is to get those schools open again.

A Pennsylvania judge agrees:

> Courts of equity have the power and duty to require that board action conform to the public interest. The public interest is that of conducting a good school system; not that of achieving greater participation of teachers' organizations in school policy, or that of maintaining unfettered control of school affairs by local boards of education, or that of establishing the highest or lowest possible salary schedules, or that of exempting from or imposing upon professional employees noninstructional duties, or, finally, that of nourishing or weakening employee associations.[17]

Indeed, a judge may find that the actions of both parties are open to criticism and that the real "losers" in the dispute are not those at the bargaining table but the students. A Michigan Court stated:

> It becomes increasingly apparent that the board would rather discipline its teachers than educate its students. This fact is not altered by the union's similar pursuit of its selfish interests at the children's expense. The board's punitive conduct at the children's expense is arbitrary and unreasonable. Being unreasonable, it is unconstitutional as a deprivation of the students' right to due process.[18]

A judge in Pennsylvania noted that in the adjudication of a teacher strike, "No one really represents the interest of the students, who are the beneficiaries or victims of the dispute."[19] And another notes that in teacher-strike cases, ''Children are· pawns in an adult game of economics.''[20]

The Moment of Decision

Given the external situation pressures and the other considerations that the judge must weigh and given the situation that the judge has decided not to issue an injunction immediately, what options are available?

One option is for the judge to simply delay the case and hope that the parties will resolve the matter on their own. A New York Public Employee Relations Board attorney refers to instances he observed:

> I've known some lawyers that have had trouble finding judges who will sign orders, such injunction orders. Some judges, I suspect, aren't interested in getting involved in this kind of thing. They're hard to locate when it comes to signing an order to enjoin a strike. . . . A day or two or three may go by before an order is obtained.

On the other hand, a judge may find some way to distinguish a particular strike from other recent strikes. If the judge can find the current strike unique, then the case need not be decided with reference to previous cases and a judge is more free to tailor a result he or she believes is just. A Michigan teacher attorney generalizes from his long experience:

> But if the court takes the case and reviews it, I would have absolutely no idea what argument they might find of significance. . . . Very frequently, you know, in these cases with political overtones, the courts think it's much safer to go off on some very rather minor and obscure technical point that's fairly bereft of emotional content. And so they'll pick that up . . . and say, ''Well, we're just sorry . . . , we certainly think you were right in slamming all these teachers or whatever. But you just didn't do it right. You forgot such and such a statutory provision or you should have given more notice than you did or some such thing.

Or judges may perceive that additional bargaining between the parties will resolve the matter. Then the most direct and expedient action is to order bargaining. In doing so, the judge may carefully fine-tune both his own involvement in the case and the kind of sanctions that will be involved if the parties fail to reach agreement. A Washington judge was presented with a request for a temporary restraining order. He issued an order restraining picketing but indicated that he was not prepared to enjoin the strike itself at that point. He continued:

I am going to order negotiations to commence. There will be at least ten hours of negotiations conducted by both parties prior to 9:00 o'clock Monday morning when I will talk with the negotiator. . . . I am hesitant to try to use the powers of the court to issue an injunction as a tool for either party in the negotiation proceeding.[21]

Four days later, when the case was still pending, the judge did issue the temporary restraining order against the strike. And he enlarged his own involvement in the case. He noted that as he listened to the parties, he had become persuaded that he should issue a supplemental order to involve the court in a monitoring of the bargaining, to review charges of "bad faith," and to use the powers of the court to achieve an agreement. Though not anxious to become more directly involved, he noted that he would be open to a request from either party to participate in a "settlement conference" or other form of supervised negotiation. Thus the judge gradually escalated his own involvement in the case.[22] The pattern noted in the 1978–1979 teacher-strike cases, in which judges directed or themselves became involved in negotiations represents an adaptation by the courts to the exigencies of the teacher-strike situation. If direct negotiations will ultimately resolve the strike, then a logical move is for the court to see that negotiations (under added pressure and judicial direction with judicial sanctions pending) take place. This is a form of "bargaining in the shadow of law"[23] and is somewhat akin to plea bargaining in criminal cases and settlement under the auspices of the court in civil cases. It is also consistent with principles of equity in which the judge is given great discretion to fashion an equitable solution. However, there are counterindications to ordering bargaining. A Washington judge explains:

It has been urged upon this Court that it intervene directly in the negotiating process. This Court is not unmindful of what has been done in other jurisdictions of this State. . . . In my opinion, however, at this point in time to have this Court involve itself or persons appointed by it directly into the negotiation process would simply insert new and additional parties into that process—whether you call them "Masters," or "Fact-Finders," or "Intermediators," or whatever—who would have to be brought up to date to such an extent about the issues involved and all of the facts surrounding those issues and the positions of the parties, that it would not enhance negotiations but would, in fact, tend to impede or delay them.[24]

Further, in a recent Missouri case, an appellate court ruled that a trial-court judge had exceeded his jurisdiction in ordering bargaining. The lower-court judge had specified:

It is further ordered that the parties meet and confer in good faith in an attempt to resolve the present salary dispute which led to the alleged current work stoppage. This court recognizes that neither party has any obligation per se to compromise during these discussions.

However, the appellate court held that such an order was a mandatory injunction.

A mandatory injunction is a harsh remedy and is to be granted by a court only when the right thereto is clearly established. It should never be granted on doubtful proof. . . . Without question, the trial judge was attempting in good faith to help resolve a controversy important to a large segment of the public, but courts should not act as mediators in labor disputes. Generally the courts will not interfere with the exercise of a school district's discretion except in a case of clear abuse, fraud, or some similar conduct.[25]

The appeals court further noted that there was no parallel between private- and public-sector negotiations and that "many of the problems of public employee pay discussions arise out of a failure to recognize the major legal differences between public and private employees."

It will be remembered from previous chapters that boards sometimes do not support judicial direction of bargaining, partly because they perceive it as infringing on the prerogatives of the board. Further, although teacher groups may support such bargaining because it brings the dispute back to the table where the real differences are, teacher attorneys may also question the legal basis for such intervention:

He [the judge] would have one of us locked up along with both sides to assist the court and both sides in reaching some kind of agreement. I question whether or not that was legally correct to do so. Could he, himself, act as the super arbitrator? He was really not looking for final and binding agreement but he was using the pressures of his bench to force a settlement, to get both sides to move towards the middle to an agreement. . . . I don't know whether the judge really has that kind of authority to do that. . . . No one has ever challenged him, either side, that I know of. . . , it's always served the purpose of resolving the dispute and having an agreement ultimately be negotiated and signed. . . . I think some employer group or employee group is going to test the propriety of the judge's intervention. In the purest sense of the word, I think the judge is there to decide the legal issues which are presented and to do nothing more than that. . . . We've supported it because it ultimately seems to get the job done.

Should judges be tempted to go beyond ordering bargaining and/or issuing injunctions, the probabilities that their action will be reversed by a higher court rise. Illinois and Pennsylvania courts have ruled that judges may not impose any judicial settlement on a strike. The Illinois court held:

> The Court's authority to enjoin the unlawful, in this case a strike by public employees, does not carry with it any power in the Court to impose the Court's solution to the cause of the strike.[26]

A Missouri court ruled that a trial court had exceeded its jurisdiction in prohibiting the district from terminating the employment of teachers because of peaceful strike activities.[27] Hence, the judge must tread a careful path between moving the case along toward resolution and moving too far and too fast, only to be checked by a higher court. So the judge issues a decision (or embarks on a course of decisions). If this results in a resolution or if the party or parties ordered to alter their actions obey, then the role of the judge in the case is ended. No further judicial duty remains. But if the case again returns to the courts, the judicial role continues.

Contempt

When teachers defy court orders, they are continuing to treat the dispute before the court as the original bargaining-table dispute. They are continuing to assert the power of noncooperation in order to force concessions in negotiations.

Given the current high rate of defiance of court orders in public-sector strikes, judges realize the possibility (or even probability) of non-compliance by teachers. How does a judge act in the face of such possible defiance?

One strategy is to be as fair and patient and evenhanded as possible in the injunction proceedings. This may give more solid grounds for harsh action if that is deemed necessary later on. Another strategy for the judge is to assume there will be compliance. A Washington teacher attorney notes that the judge in one strike case refused to include in the injunctive order any discussion of noncompliance. The attorney relates:

> The judge didn't want any part of that. She said, "Look, I'm going to issue my order on the assumption that everybody will obey the order. I haven't heard anything to the contrary. If my order isn't obeyed then the school district can come back in and we'll see what we can do about that." She absolutely was not going to listen to any discussion of fines or penalties.

In this case, the teachers returned to work when so ordered.

In an injunction proceeding, the judge issues the order but the board decides (initially, at least) whether to enforce it. If the board does not act, the judge may take note. In a Washington case, a teacher attorney reports, judges let it be known that the school board in question "was going to have a hard time getting injunctive relief again, because it was obvious that they really weren't interested in an injunction, they were interested in getting some tool in negotiations. Otherwise they would have come back in for contempt."

Subsequently, a judge in a more recent case in the same district gave reasons for his actions in delaying an injunction:

> An injunction is the exercise of extraordinary power by the judicial branch of the government. . . , and that takes me back to Judge *M*'s order. . . . It disturbs me from the standpoint that the order was entered, publicized, apparently was ignored by everybody, the school district, the school teachers, the association. Certainly, it is not this court's policy to issue injunctions if it feels that they are going to be ignored by both parties. . . . I will consider entering such an injunction next week but as a condition to my consideration of that, it will be necessary for the district to submit to the court a plan as to how this injunction is to be served and become effective; how it is to be monitored as to compliance, and what position the plaintiff will take with respect to an attempt to bargain away any violations of the injunction in the process of negotiations with the association. To do less than that in my view will result in the same type of situation that occurred with Judge *M*'s order and other court orders in the past that have been disregarded. In this particular context that can do nothing more than breed a contempt of the law already rampant in our society.[28]

A legal order ceases to function as law if it is widely disregarded. Judges reserve some of their sharpest comments in the cases we examined for those who defy their orders: A New York judge asserted:

> Transcending in importance defendants' violation of our statutes is the fact that in doing so they have deliberately defied the lawful mandate of the Court. The defendant Union, powerful though it may be, is nevertheless insufficiently powerful to disdain, with impunity, the law and the Court. Our existence as a free people is dependent on a healthy respect for law and order. For ours is a society open and ordered, animate and free, and it can continue so only so long as we maintain our liberties *under law*. Ironic indeed is the fact that this basic lesson in elementary civics must be taught anew to, of all pupils, the very persons to whom we daily entrust our tender offspring for training and development as the leaders of tomorrow.[29]

In the 1978 Memphis teachers strike, Chancellor D.J. Alissandratos lectured teachers at the conclusion of the hearing on contempt:

Judges are servants of our rule of law and not the law itself, and must stand prepared and determined to do their duty and punish all violators of the law. You have the free will to obey the law of civilized society or to break that law. Because you are free to choose, you should not be protected from yourselves nor the consequences of your actions. Under our system of the rule of law, the judiciary has exclusive authority to arbitrate disputes. . . . The courtroom is the battleground for any such disputes and not the streets. . . . No one anywhere along the way may disregard the controlling court's ruling, for whatever reason, and certainly not because it does not suit them, and if any person chooses to disregard such rulings they must fully expect to be punished. . . . You expect to have authority in your classrooms as delegated to you by the law, but you deny the constitutional authority of your judicial system. . . . You have made the bed, and it is this court's duty to see that you lie in it.

He then sentenced nine teacher leaders to serve ten days in the Shelby jail. But he also lectured school-board members:

This is a court of equity, and I therefore will apply the equitable principle that "one who seeks equity must do equity." . . . [This court] expects the school board to shoulder its share of the responsibility and assist the court in putting an end to this illegal strike. The school board has a greater power than this court in that it has the power to fire those who refuse to report for work. This court cannot, has not, and will not order people back to work, but it has ordered them not to continue an illegal strike, and if, by the 21st you have not exercised your power to irrevocably fire those who do not report for work, then I consider you to be acting in bad faith with this court and will consider dissolving this injunction and take such failure in account in assessing any fines. . . . I am not going to ease up on either side. You are going to do what is right and there is not going to be any using the courts to jockey for negotiation leverage. To both sides I would say, if you get no other message, get this. No one, no group, is above the law. Lawlessness will not be tolerated by this court and the law will prevail.[30]

Predicting Judicial Behavior

Given the complexities of the legal rules and the facts of the case, the social and political pressures on the judge and the court's own assessment of the efficacy of the injunctive process in reaching a resolution of the dispute, it is not surprising that judges proceed with care and caution in the handling of teacher-strike cases. And given the broad complex of variables that may influence the judicial decision, it is not surprising that parties and observers of teacher-strike cases find it difficult to predict what a judge may do or say.

A Michigan attorney who has argued many strike cases for teachers, comments on the factors that may influence the judge:

> The essential *ad hoc* quality of many judicial decisions is nowhere more evident than in teacher-strike situations. Courts invariably consider the degree of community support or condemnation of the strikers, what the court presumes, usually without any evidence, to be the threat to educational processes, the political expediency of Draconian restraints or temporizing delays and other factors rehearsed by Jerome Frank and the other legal realists more than a generation ago. Very rarely in my experience has there been any discussion of what is meant by "irreparable injury" in judicial opinions, and even in those cases I would hold the recitals extremely suspect. In this area, what judges say may have little relationship to what judges do.

Another Michigan teacher attorney who has handled many teacher-strike cases also indicates prediction of judicial behavior is difficult:

> It's very difficult to tell sometimes what factors really are influencing the judge. Everybody likes to think that somehow, the law and the judges work in a very scientific manner. But the fact of the matter is they don't, particularly when you get into this area where they have a great deal of discretion whether or not to issue an injunction. It can depend on his values. The judge may just have a philosophical bent that he doesn't like unions, he doesn't like strikes, he clearly doesn't like illegal strikes. And frankly, what is the makeup of his constitutents? You get down into the Wayne County area, where you've got a very heavy labor population. You've got a lot of people used to being on strikes. You've got elected judges. You're going to be elected by these people. The judge may not want to be perceived as antilabor. And he's going to quite often be a little more leery about finding irreparable damage in issuing the injunction. It gets right down to such things sometimes as how busy is the judge? Is he right in the middle of a great big jury trial? Or at this particular point when this thing's coming up, maybe his schedule isn't quite as bad and he feels, "Well, I've got a little more time to cajole the parties and try to get an agreement." There's all of these factors that come in here. And quite often you never really know what is motivating him either to grant or not grant an injunction. You just never know. . . . Rarely does a judge ever argue or ever rule, "I find no irreparable damage." What he simply does is hold off giving the injunction. And he gets the parties and says, "Well, now, let's see here, before we continue this I want to see the counsel back in my chambers."

And a Michigan "expert witness" who has testified on behalf of teachers in court agrees that what influences a judge is difficult to assess:

> The judges seem not to pay very much attention to real evidence. The opinion seems to be that they pretty much have their minds made up

ahead of time, what they're going to do about an injunction. And the best we've been able to do, and I think what most of the attorneys are really hoping will happen is for the judge to delay his order. . . . My hunch is they're motivated more by the political damage that can happen to them if they refuse to enjoin. . . . It's a no-win situation for those guys.

Judges seem to get the feel or Gestalt of a case, which is then embedded in the entire context of decision: The law, the facts, the political realities, the societal pressures. They know what they must decide in the light of these factors. They may then seize on some bit of the evidence presented before them which, for them, demonstrates the rightness of their decision. For one judge, it was the testimony that a high school student had been seen carrying a sign that said "Fire my teacher." For the judge, this symbolized the harm occurring because of the strike and was an indication of why it must be enjoined. For another, a "particularly poignant affidavit" on the damage caused by discontinuity in the remedial training of children with cleft palates and speech defects dramatized the deleterious effects of the strike.

The inability to predict with reliability what the judge will do and when he or she will do it is one of the factors cited by parties that lead them to avoid taking the case to court. On the other hand, it is apparent that judges are presented with complex problems in teacher strikes. Their settlement attempts and their encouragement toward return to the bargaining table represent a pragmatic, problem-solving approach to the dilemmas they find. And while some parties view these efforts with skepticism and disfavor, other parties welcome the assistance because "it gets the job done." Parties expressing high satisfaction with their recent court experience in 1978–1979 are more than twice as likely to have received such settlement assistance than were parties indicating only some satisfaction.

Karl N. Lewellyn, commenting on the task of the courts, noted that "this doing of something about disputes, this doing of it reasonably, is the business of law."[31] And this is what many of these judges are about.

Notes

1. Order Granting Temporary Restraining Order, *Everett School District No. 2 v. Everett Education Association,* No. 78-2-02952-1, Super. Ct., Snohomish County, Wash. (September 19, 1978).

2. Bernard C. Brominski, "Limited Right to Strike Laws—Can

They Work When Applied to Public Education? From the Perspective of the Local Judge,'' *Journal of Law and Education* 2 (1973):677–688.

3. *Bellefonte Area Education Association v. Board of Education,* Pa. Commw., 304 A.2d. 922 (1973):923.

4. Oral Decision of the Court, *Central Kitsap School District No. 401 v. Central Kitsap Education Association,* No. 78-2-00607-0, Super. Ct., Kitsap Co., Wash. (September 6, 1978):3.

5. Brominski, ''Limited Right to Strike,'' p. 686.

6. Supplemental Opinion of the Court, *Armstrong School District v. Armstrong Education Association,* No. 226, June Term, 1971 (C.P. Armstrong Co., September 14, 1971):2.

7. *Bristol Township Education Association v. School District,* Pa. Commw., 322 A.2d. 767 (1974):773–774.

8. *State of Delaware v. Delaware State Educational Association,* Del. Ch. 326 A.2d. 868 (1974):875.

9. Philippe Nonet and Philip Selznick, *Law and Society in Transition: Toward Responsive Law* (New York: Colophon Books, Harper and Row, 1978), pp. 60–67.

10. *School District v. Education Association,* 79 LRRM 2455 (Pa. C.P., York Co., 1971):2456.

11. *City and County of San Francisco v. Cooper,* 534 P.2d. 403 (1975):412.

12. Charles Redenius, ''Public Employees: A Survey of Some Critical Problems on the Frontier of Collective Bargaining,'' *Labor Law Journal* 27 (September 1976):588–599.

13. *Central Kitsap School District No. 401,* p. 4–5.

14. Order Granting Injunction, *Butler Area School District v. Butler Education Association,* No. 78-002, C.P., Butler Co., Pa. (January 1978):149.

15. *Central Kitsap No. 401,* p. 8.

16. *State v. Delaware,* p. 876.

17. *Root v. Northern Cambria School District,* Pa. Commw., 309 A.2d. 175 (1973):177.

18. Brief in Support of Complaint for Mandamus, *Irwin v. Ecorse Board of Education,* No. 118598, Cir. Ct., Wayne County, Mich. (September 26, 1968).

19. *Bristol Township v. School District,* p. 774.

20. *Bellefonte Area v. Board of Education,* p. 926.

21. *Everett No. 2 v. Everett Education Association,* pp. 11–12.

22. Id. at 2.

23. Robert H. Mnookin and Lewis Kornhauser, ''Bargaining in the

Shadow of Law: The Case of Divorce,'' *Yale Law Journal* 88 (April 1979):950–997.

24. Order Granting Temporary Injunction, *Tacoma School District No. 10 v. Tacoma Association of Classroom Teachers,* No. 270633, Super. Ct., Pierce County, Wash. (September 29, 1978):11–13.

25. *Government Employee Relations Report* (Washington, D.C.: Bureau of National Affairs, 8 June 1981) 916:15–16; and *Parkway School District v. Provoznik,* Mo. Ct. of Appeals, 617 S.W.2d, 489 (1981).

26. *People v. Board of Education,* 96 LRRM 2412 (Ill. Cir. Ct., 6th Cir., 1971):2412.

27. *Kansas City School District v. Clymer,* 96 LRRM 2945 (Mo. Ct. App., 1977):2947.

28. *Everett No. 2 v. Everett Education Association,* pp. 8–10.

29. *Board of Education of City of New York v. Shanker,* 283 N.Y.W.2d. 548 (October 4, 1967):553.

30. ''Text of Chancellor D.J. Alissandratos' Lecture to Striking Memphis Teachers on Obeying the Law,'' *Government Employee Relations Report* (Washington, D.C.: Bureau of National Affairs, October 23, 1978) 782:26–29.

31. Karl N. Llewellyn, *The Bramble Bush* (New York: Oceana Publication, 1960), p. 3.

7 Summary and Conclusions

Since midcentury teachers' dissatisfaction with their economic status and working conditions has bred levels and forms of militance previously unknown in public-sector employment. Emulating practices developed in private-sector labor-management relations, teachers have promoted unionism, advocated the practice of collective bargaining, and conducted strikes. The courts have become involved in the last of these developments whenever school boards have sought injunctive relief from teacher strikes.

Injunction proceedings raise questions not merely about the legality of teacher strikes; they also direct attention to the nature of the courts' equity powers and to the courts' role in the resolution of social disputes. In the preceding chapters, we examined the injunctive process in detail. We now consider the strengths and limitations of current policies and practices affecting court involvement in teacher strikes.

Initially it is necessary to delimit the terms of discourse. First, we are not assessing the desirability of collective bargaining per se. Discussion of the costs and benefits of bargaining for children, teachers, school officials, and the general public is amply presented elsewhere.[1] For our purposes, it is sufficient to note that, desirable or not, collective bargaining today is widespread in the public schools.

Second, while we readily acknowledge that the growth of collective bargaining has been accompanied by growth in the incidence of teacher strikes, we reject the contention that collective bargaining "causes" teacher strikes. As we noted in chapter 2, the roots of teacher strikes are complex and varied. Well over 90 percent of the collective contracts between teachers and school boards are negotiated without strikes. The bargaining process is implicated directly in some strikes, indirectly in others, and not at all in still others.

Third, it is useful to distinguish between policies concerning teacher strikes and policies concerning injunctive relief from teacher strikes. Some statutes and some school boards create a direct connection; strikes automatically trigger requests for injunctive relief. Other states and other school boards make the connection a contingent one: Strikes elicit requests for injunctive relief under some circumstances but not others. In still other situations the possibility of seeking injunctive relief from a strike is not even considered.

Finally, in thinking about the policies pertaining to injunctive relief from teacher strikes, it is useful to look beyond the immediate issues that arise in court. The organizational dynamics of courts, school boards, and teacher associations, and the larger social contexts in which these organizations function cannot be ignored. For although litigation ostensibly isolates legal issues—lifting them out of context—the isolation is temporary and incomplete. Sooner or later legal disputes are set back into their social contexts. Moreover, the courts themselves are social settings that affect the outcomes of litigation.

Summary of Findings

The preceding chapters examined the injunction process from the perspectives of school-board petitioners, teacher respondents, and the courts. In chapter 4 we noted that school boards take into account a wide array of factors in weighing the decision about whether to seek injunctive relief. One factor is the law governing the availability of injunctive relief. Another is the possibility of judicial involvement in efforts to settle the underlying dispute. Power relationships also are considered: How will injunction proceedings affect the teachers' capacity to continue their strike, and how will it affect the support of various constituencies? A subsidiary set of questions arises in connection with the injunctive process itself. Legal proceedings involve new actors, new procedures, and new issues; their relationships to the underlying teacher-board dispute and ensuing strike pose complex questions of legal strategy and tactics.

Teachers, who seized the initiative in calling a strike, are respondents in court. Once a board has filed for injunctive relief, the teachers must devise strategies for protecting their strike from being enjoined and for shaping injunction proceedings in ways that contribute to a negotiated settlement of the underlying dispute. Teacher attorneys try to invoke traditional limitations upon the courts' capacity to issue injunctions, thereby gaining precious hours or days in which pressures toward settlement can be applied against the board of education. In addition, teachers often become willing participants in court-initiated or court-supported efforts to settle the bargaining issues. Where injunctions are issued, teachers more often than not defy them, hoping that such defiance, even if penalized, will help induce negotiations.

Faced with the choice of accepting the board's contention that the problem is an illegal strike or the teachers' contention that the problem is an underlying employment dispute, operating in a context of ambiguous and inconsistent case law and statutory law, and subject to the emotionalism of a strike that may disrupt an entire community, judges respond in a variety of ways. Some act decisively on behalf of school-board claims. Some delay, hoping that the underlying problem will be settled without judicial involvement. Some insist on the application of sanctions for noncompliance with injunctions; others are happy to see the strike settled and the case dismissed. Many courts, we found, actively promote efforts to negotiate settlement of the teacher–board dispute. Thus some courts act on the petitioners' definition of the situation. Some courts accept the respondents' view. Some courts do nothing. But a common response is to accept both the petitioners' *and* the respondents' arguments—enjoining the strike and directing negotiations.

Trends

Our conversations with veterans in the field of school labor–management relations and our review of previous studies of teacher strikes suggest that there is a trend away from major reliance on injunctions as strike-ending devices. The trend has several roots. One lies in changes in the law. Several legislatures and courts have restricted the availability of injunctive relief in teacher strikes. By 1981 seven state legislatures had adopted statutes giving teachers a limited right to strike and allowing injunctions only under restricted circumstances. In addition, there are a few states where the courts themselves have taken steps to limit the availability of injunctive relief. In its 1968 *Holland* decision the Michigan Supreme Court held that mere illegality was not a sufficient justification for awarding injunctive relief; traditional equitable standards—clean hands, irreparable harm, exhaustion of administrative remedies—also had to be considered. Illinois courts rarely grant *ex parte* orders. In California the 1979 *San Diego* decision created a *de facto* right to strike by establishing that a board seeking injunctive relief must apply to PERB to determine whether the strike constitutes an unfair labor practice. If so, PERB (not the school board) should determine what remedies, if any, it should pursue. If none are pursued, the strike could continue without legal action.

Statutory and judicial limitations on the availability of injunctive relief have weakened one of the classic sources of an injunction's potency. Swiftness and surprise simply are not possible if an employer is precluded from obtaining an injunction in the few critical hours immediately before or after the beginning of a strike. The traditional scenario, in which strike leaders are served with court orders just as they are preparing for a strike vote or deploying pickets, is no longer possible in a number of states. Instead, the strike is well launched, and there must be a public hearing before injunctive relief becomes available. In some instances the delay between the beginning of a strike and the availability of relief may extend over several days or even weeks.

A second factor limiting the use of injunctions is found in new developments in school-board strategic planning. As the incidence of teacher strikes has increased, school managers have learned that striking teachers are not revolutionary brigades and that closed schools do not bring instant community chaos. Strike manuals now teach school managers that it is possible to "take" a strike by hiring substitutes to keep the schools open, by dismissal threats, by decertification proceedings, and by appeals to the public for patience and support. Thus injunctive relief is simply one option among many, its use to be dictated by its fit with other tactics and by the stage of development of the strike itself. Injunctions may, for example, be invoked merely to limit picketing. Requests for relief may be delayed until school managers are persuaded that teacher solidarity is collapsing, at which point an injunction may provide teachers with a face-saving device for terminating the stoppage. Injunction proceedings may be orchestrated with settlement efforts so as to exert maximum pressure on teachers.

Experience has played a part in the evolution of school-board strike strategy. School boards have learned that injunctions are not panaceas. Sometimes they do more harm than good by enhancing teacher solidarity and morale. Injunctions can be defied, thus requiring enforcement proceedings that may make poststrike reconciliations more difficult. Injunctions can lead to judicial intervention on behalf of settlement efforts, even if the board prefers to hold out against the teachers.

Despite growing statutory and judicial restrictions on the use of labor injunctions in teacher strikes, and despite growing awareness by school managers that injunctions may have limited potency and undesirable side-effects, there is support for their continued availability and use. Gallup polls show that whereas public support for giving teachers a right to strike grew from 37 percent in 1969 to 45 percent in 1975, the support dropped to 40 percent in 1980.[2] Support for teacher bargaining itself may be eroding; one major advocate of teacher bargaining recently has shifted his position.[3] Thus there is no clear consensus to guide policymakers.

Policy Alternatives and Adjustments

Teacher strikes are not picnics. They are arduous affairs not merely for the teachers and school managers directly involved but also for the students, parents, and communities affected. Children may cheer about "days off," teachers may sing songs of solidarity, and otherwise-fractious school boards may attain new levels of unity and resolve in the face of a strike. But these facades cannot conceal the fact that the social fabric has been torn. Virtually everyone contends that some other strategy of dispute resolution would be preferable to a strike. No one contests the idea that the incidence and impact of teacher strikes ought to be minimized. It is the means, not the goals, that are at issue.

Efforts to control teacher strikes can (and do) take a variety of forms. They need not involve the courts. Punitive statutes can be designed, imposing fines on striking teachers, decertifying their bargaining units, or automatically dismissing strikers. Preventive measures can be adopted, ameliorating the sources of teacher and board militance, improving the skill of bargaining teams, and introducing impasse mechanisms such as mediation and arbitration. Bargaining can be banned. We are not in a position to assess such mechanisms as we did not examine them. Our research suggests that such mechanisms warrant the broadest possible exploration because the courts, by themselves, have only limited efficacy in controlling the incidence and impact of strikes.

Contemporary policies concerning the courts' role appear to be drifting in contradictory directions. Some states attempt to maximize the deterrent and punitive powers of the courts by requiring struck school boards to seek injunctive relief, by removing traditional equitable limitations on the issuance of injunctions, by limiting the courts' capacity to foster settlement efforts, and by insisting on harsh punishment of those who violate injunctions. However, there are other states that restrict petitioners' access to injunctive relief, reserving such relief for situations in which the public interest is seriously jeopardized. Such is the situation in the several states where there are "limited right-to-strike" statutes and in those states where the courts have used injunctive relief selectively instead of automatically. Each of these policies, we suggest, is based primarily on consideration of the deterrent power of injunctions. None recognize the courts' potentialities for actively fostering settlement of the social dispute underlying the strike.

Deterrence

The customary rationale for making injunctions readily accessible to school boards is that injunctions deter strikes. The deterrent value of an injunction is presumed to arise from several factors. One is that potential strikers otherwise willing to test a board's mettle may be deterred by the awesome prospect of having to fight the courts as well. Litigation consumes time and resources. It diverts attention from the underlying teacher–board dispute. Another feature of the courts' deterrent power is that judicially imposed sanctions can be severe; fines and jail sentences can be meted out, and individuals can be exposed to the opprobrium associated with the status of lawbreakers. In addition, a loss in court may cause loss of public support that is needed to apply pressure to the board of education. In each of these ways injunctions can increase the cost (to teachers) of a strike, thereby reducing its likelihood or heightening teacher receptivity to the board's terms for settling the underlying dispute. Put differently, the deterrent value of injunctions rests on their capacity to alter power relationships between teachers and school boards.

The deterrent value of injunctions is real, but it also is limited. Some strikes are prevented by injunctions. Some strikes are ended by injunctions. Some settlements are induced by the pendency of injunction proceedings and sanctions. However, many strikes occur in spite of court orders barring them, and some continue even in the face of massive fines and teacher jailings.

The reasons for the limited deterrent value of injunctions are apparent in our findings. School-board petitioners often discover obstacles on the road to injunctive relief. While eventual courtroom success is probable, the intervening problems—the delays and the unsought side-effects— substantially lessen the deterrent value of injunctions. Moreover, even if issued by a court, an injunction may not be sufficiently potent to overcome teacher determination to continue their strike while absorbing judicially imposed sanctions. Injunctions may even heighten that determination.

The difficulties encountered by petitioners do not demonstrate failures of the legal process. They reflect its vitality. The courts are not supposed to allocate power arbitrarily between petitioners and respondents; they are supposed to allocate power fairly. That requires at least a minimal opportunity for both sides to be heard. It requires at least a minimal acknowledgment of long-established limitations on judicial power. As we have seen, teachers take full advantages of opportunities to be heard, and they ask the courts to adhere to traditional limitations on the use of injunctions. Denial of such opportunities would violate enduring principles of the legal system.

More than half a century ago Felix Frankfurter and Nathan Greene published their treatise on judicial abuse of equitable powers in the issuance of labor injunctions.[4] Such abuse, the treatise warned, undermined the legitimacy of the courts and threatened the rule of law. Our observations of injunction proceedings accompanying teacher strikes suggest that in a substantial proportion of injunction proceedings, there is at least a rudimentary effort to assure that both sides are heard and that traditional limitations on the courts' injunctive powers are at least considered. Thus the remedies proposed by Frankfurter and Greene—drastic curtailment of the courts' jurisdiction over labor–management disputes—may not be warranted in the case of teacher strikes. Despite occasional statutes and court decisions that have the effect of making injunctions easily available to school boards, the dominant trend is toward limiting the utilization of injunctions and toward recognition of the validity of traditional limitations on the courts' injunctive powers. Some of these limitations arise in the legal system. Even as our research was under way in 1979, one state—California—was the scene of litigation that had the effect of limiting the availability of injunctive relief.[5] Another state—Minnesota—subsequently joined the ranks of those that statutorily curtail the use of injunctions by legalizing teacher strikes.[6]

As previously noted, limits on the use of injunctions also are a consequence of management decisions to stay out of court. The school districts that stayed out of court in the 1978–1979 strikes did so, in part, because they were not confident that injunctive relief would be awarded, were not sure that teachers would obey an injunction, and were worried about the undesirable side-effects of injunction proceedings. In short, these districts recognized the limited nature of the deterrent power of injunctions. Contemporary school management literature warns school boards of these limits. In effect, injunction proceedings that give respondents an opportunity to be heard and that give courts an opportunity to exercise discretion, render the outcomes less certain and the process less desirable from the petitioner's viewpoint.

Ironically, recognition of the limited deterrent value of injunctions could enhance the effectiveness of injunction proceedings that do occur. School boards that rush into court in the opening moments of a strike sometimes find their petitions rebuffed or the courts' orders defied; boards that wait longer may find more receptive judges and an increased likelihood of teacher compliance. This is not to say that precipitous action always fails or that considered action always succeeds. Our data are too limited to permit comparisons between cases in which injunctions were quickly sought and readily granted and cases in which injunctions were sought on a delayed basis and obtained only after a hearing. However, as a general proposition, we suggest that deliberation and fairness are important correlates of judicial efficacy. The same proposition may apply to injunctions in teacher strikes.

There is another reason for thinking that it may be wiser to preserve the limited availability of injunctions and to encourage full use of the courts' equitable powers rather than to remove the courts' jurisdiction over labor–management disputes or to make injunctions more easily available. Our observations suggest that the courts can do more than deter strikes. They can—and do—help settle them.

Dispute Resolution

In case after case we found that injunction proceedings elicited judicial efforts to facilitate resolution of the underlying teacher–board disputes. Judges did not limit their activities to consideration of the legal issues associated with petitioners' requests for injunctive relief. They fostered settlement efforts. The parties sometimes were directed to engage in bargaining. Injunction proceedings often were delayed in order to furnish opportunities for the parties to settle their differences. On occasion courts directly intervened in settlements, as in Washington, D.C., where the court not merely enjoined the teachers' strike but also reinstituted an expired teacher contract.[7] A Connecticut judge called on a judicial colleague to function as a mediator.[8]

The fact of such efforts is hardly surprising if we consider the normal operations of the courts. Most litigation is never brought to trial or final judgment. The courts serve as forums and levers in the resolution of all sorts of social conflicts. The existence of a legal dispute simply provides a pretext for being in court. Once there, there are strong pressures on the parties to settle their differences before a judicial determination of the legal issues is rendered. The reasons are not hard to find. Litigation is tedious and costly with the result that the parties and the courts themselves have an incentive to settle differences short of full adjudication. Moreover, the uncertainty principle is at work: The risk of an adverse judicial decision may be higher than the costs of mutual agreement. Thus judicially sponsored settlement efforts may be as welcome as adjudication of the legal dispute.

This is not to say that the courts are optimum forums for the resolution of teacher–board disputes. Using the courts in this manner ties up institutions that might better be used to deal with other types of social problems. The process is also expensive. Moreover, not all judges are skilled in the process of dispute resolution, and not all of them are neutral in their view of teacher–board disputes. Some are prolabor; some are promanagement. Some know the problems of education very well; others are poorly informed. Few are specialists in labor–management problems. It is conceivable that other agencies—labor courts, for example—could be designed to perform the same function in a more expert manner. But for the moment the trial courts are what we have. Their limitations are real, but so are their potentialities in the area of dispute resolution.

What we are suggesting, in short, is that injunction proceedings serve two functions, not one. The courts can help deter strikes. And the courts can help settle strikes. But they cannot perform both functions if policymakers view the courts merely as punitive agencies that should automatically be allied with one side in a teacher–board dispute. Through the exercise of the full powers of equity, the courts may best realize their potential in serving the larger social purpose of controlling teacher strikes.

Notes

1. Anthony M. Cresswell and Michael J. Murphy, *Teachers, Unions, and Collective Bargaining in Public Education* (Berkeley, Calif.: McCutchan Publishing, 1980); Richard P. Schick and Jean J. Couturier, *The Public Interest in Government Labor Relations* (Cambridge, Mass.: Ballinger, 1977); Lorraine McDonnell and Anthony Pascal, *Organized Teachers in American Schools* (Santa Monica, Calif.: RAND, R-2407-NIE, 1979); and Myron Lieberman, *Public Sector Bargaining* (Lexington, Mass.: Lexington Books, D.C. Heath, 1980).

2. Stanley M. Elam, *A Decade of Gallup Polls of Attitudes Toward Education, 1969–1978* (Bloomington, Ind.: Phi Delta Kappa, 1978), pp. 35, 238; and George H. Gallup, "The 12th Annual Gallup Poll of the Public's Attitudes Toward Public Schools," *Phi Delta Kappan* 62 (September 1980):40.

3. Myron Lieberman, "Eggs That I Have Laid: Teacher Bargaining Reconsidered," *Phi Delta Kappan* 60 (February 1979):415–419.

4. Felix Frankfurter and Nathan Greene, *The Labor Injunction* (New York: Macmillan, 1930).

5. *San Diego Teachers Association v. Superior Court*, 154 Cal. Rptr. 893, Cal. Sup. Ct. (1979).

6. *Cuebook II: State Education Collective Bargaining Laws*, Report No. F80-5 (Denver: Education Commission of the States, 1980).

7. Memorandum Opinion and Order, *Vincent Reed et al. v. Washington Teachers' Union*, C.A. No. 2534-79, Super. Ct. of the District of Columbia (March 28, 1979).

8. *Bridgeport* (Conn.) *Post*, September 12, 1978.

Appendix:
State Statutes
Pertaining to Teacher
Bargaining and Strikes,
1980

1. Bargaining authorized; strikes prohibited (N = 19)

Connecticut	Maine	New York
Delaware	Maryland	North Dakota
Florida	Massachusetts	Oklahoma
Indiana	Michigan	Rhode Island
Iowa	Nebraska	South Dakota
Kansas	Nevada	Tennessee
	New Hampshire	

2. Bargaining authorized; limited strikes permitted (N = 7)

Alaska	Minnesota	Wisconsin
Hawaii	Oregon	Vermont
	Pennsylvania	

3. Bargaining authorized; no mention of strikes (N = 5)

California	Montana	Washington
Idaho	New Jersey	

4. Bargaining not authorized; strikes prohibited (N = 3)

Ohio	Texas	Virginia

5. Bargaining not authorized; no mention of strikes (N = 16)

Alabama	Illinois	North Carolina
Arizona	Kentucky	South Carolina
Arkansas	Louisiana	Utah
Colorado	Mississippi	West Virginia
Georgia	Missouri	Wyoming
	New Mexico	

Adapted from David L. Colton, "Statutory Provisions for Injunctive Relief in Teacher Strikes," mimeographed (Saint Louis: Center for the Study of Law in Education, Washington University, 1980).

Index of Names

Index of Subjects

About the Authors

David L. Colton is professor of education and director of the Center for the Study of Law in Education at Washington University, Saint Louis. He teaches in the areas of school government, policy, law, and management. The Center has conducted studies of the interactions between schools and government agencies in policy areas such as desegregation and special education, as well as in the labor-management relations area.

Edith E. Graber is assistant professor of sociology at Washington University. Her areas of specialization are the sociology of law and the history of social theory. She has conducted research at the University of Munich on Max Weber's sociology of law and has translated a Weber essay. Other research interests include police roles, privacy, and the mediation of disputes.